MY MERRY MORNINGS

Stories from Prague
by Ivan Klíma

translated by George Theiner

readers international

Title of the Czech original manuscript: *Má Veselá Jitra*.
© 1983 by Reich Publishing Company Ltd., Lucerne, Switzerland.

First published in English by Readers International, Inc., London and New York, whose editorial branch is at 8 Strathray Gardens, London NW3 4NY, England. US inquiries to 503 Broadway, 5th Floor, New York, NY 10012, USA. US Subscription and Order Department: P.O. Drawer E, Columbia, Louisiana 71418 USA.

Cover, frontispiece and illustrations by Jan Brychta

Typesetting by Red Lion Setters, London WC1N 2LA
Printed and bound in Great Britain by Richard Clay (The Chaucer Press) Ltd., Bungay, Suffolk

ISBN 0–930523–04–0   hardcover
ISBN 0–930523–05–9   softcover

MONDAY MORNING
A Black Market Tale

It was on a Monday morning that little Freddie landed on my terrace. I was sitting at my desk, writing, when suddenly I thought I could hear someone out in the hall. I could not understand it because my wife and children were long gone and I had locked the front door as usual.

"Anybody there?" I called out.

Silence.

Puzzled, I went out, and in the hall I found Freddie, standing there with a little blood and a rebellious expression on his face.

"How on earth ..! How did you get here?"

"I jumped." He was smearing the blood all over his face with his hand, but he didn't cry.

Freddie is five years old and belongs to the people upstairs in the attic apartment, which doesn't really qualify as an apartment at all. He has very dark, Jewish eyes, elongated ears, and the jaw of a pugilist—all inherited from his father. There he stood, still spreading the blood over his face, silently regarding me. Our hall is completely windowless, no way can anyone jump in there.

"You *jumped* in here?"

"I jumped out the window." Freddie has the imagination of a poet and the guile of a professional criminal. Both inherited from his father. When Freddie sees a little girl playing in the sand he pees on her back. Not that his father does *that* any more. At least, so I supposed.

"You couldn't *possibly* have jumped here from the window."

"I jumped on the terrace."

Well, I thought, he was certainly here and so it stood to reason he had to get in *somehow*. I strode through the bedroom, Freddie at my heels. The terrace was built of concrete. In the middle of it, among all the pot plants and cacti that my wife grows there, I found a brownish pool of blood. Looking up, I saw that the window just below the attic was open.

"You jumped from up there?"

"Yeah."

I couldn't understand how it was he didn't cry, but then maybe he was suffering from shock.

"Where's your daddy?"

"At work."

"And your mother?"

"She's gone shoppin'."

"Do you know where?"

"She locked me in," the boy complained, "and I was scared, so I jumped."

"Listen, Freddie, are you hurt?"

"Yeah."

"Where does it hurt?"

"Everywhere."

"Your head?"

"That too."

Now, needless to say, Freddie was no crybaby. His sadist of a father would wallop him with a leather belt and Freddie would just stand there, glaring back at him. The expression on both their faces was enough to frighten anybody. Freddie was either a brave little stoic, or he simply didn't feel any pain. One thing I knew for certain—he completely lacked the instinct of self-preservation. The first time they took him to the swimming pool, his father boasted, Freddie just darted away from them as soon as he saw the water and plunged in at the deep end. They managed to drag him out, half drowned. "But, Mr Vejr," my wife had protested when she heard this, "that's not normal. I think you should consult a psychiatrist."

"My dear lady," Freddie's father, the crook, rejected her advice, "*I* am his psychiatrist."

"Any idea when your mother's going to be back?" I asked the little stoic.

"She won't be back—she doesn't want me any more."

I was sure he was making it all up. That child didn't know when he was making something up and when, by some accident, he was actually telling the truth (just like his dad), but we couldn't very well hang around waiting for his mother to return. Not to speak of his father.

Quickly, I scribbled a message:

"Mrs Vejr,

Freddie has met with a slight accident, nothing serious. I've take him to the doctor. I'll explain when I see you."

I signed my name and pushed the piece of paper under their door upstairs.

Our house has a history of misfortunes. The local pharmacist and his wife had it built before the war for themselves and their son. The son was an officer in the gendarmerie, and after the war he fled to America. The parents were punished by being forced to move into the two-roomed attic apartment, which was not officially recognised as such because the ceilings were ten centimeters lower than the state norm prescribed. Despite this, it has always been used to house people. As if to compensate, the bathroom is almost like something out of a stately home, with tiles all the way to that unapproved ceiling. They locked the pharmacist's wife up when she was seventy years old, allegedly for selling Tuzex coupons with which people can buy foreign goods in special Tuzex shops. And of course they confiscated her half of the house. When his wife went to prison, the pharmacist—whose shop had been confiscated a long time before without his having to do anything wrong—took an overdose. He was rushed to the hospital and never came back. The wife did come back, aged seventy-three. She inherited the other half of the house and the attic apartment, to which she brought a young man who played the accordion in a night club. People said he was her lover, but I doubt if anyone really knew what their relationship was.

She called him Pepi, cooked his meals, did his washing, and bought his clothes. Pepi was an extremely quiet and polite young man, who always greeted me with the words, "Nice to see you, and please remember me to the wife." One day he just vanished. We might have come to the conclusion that someone had murdered him in the wood behind our house, which we all use as a short cut to the bus stop, if it weren't for the fact that he took his accordion and his suitcase. Six months or so later I received a postcard from him, sent from Denmark. The card showed a restaurant belonging to a Mr Hansen, and on the other side Pepi had written: "I'm doing fine and am free. Please remember me to all the tenants and to that mean old woman upstairs. Yours respectfully, Pepi."

That mean old woman upstairs lived for another five years, becoming quite senile towards the end. She was convinced everyone was out to rob her, and once a month she would phone the police to say all her savings books had been stolen. They would turn up at the house, find that everything was in order, and drive away again. When I expressed surprise that they fell for her fantasies every time, they explained that they were duty bound to investigate her complaints. What if one day it should turn out to be true?

Sad to say, they were right. But this time she did not have an opportunity to call them. We had no idea she was in there, lying quietly on her bed, until we realised that the house had been very quiet for several days. And so this time we called the police ourselves.

They got into the attic by means of a ladder from our terrace. The place stank to high heaven, and there was a large pool of dried blood on the floor. The savings books had disappeared, and the police later discovered that someone had withdrawn twenty thousand from the old lady's several bank accounts.

All the tenants were called in for questioning, about half a year after the murder. I went too, but what could I tell them? Anyway, I had formed the impression that the case didn't particularly interest them. Younger people got themselves knocked off, and the theft of a mere twenty thousand no longer impressed anyone.

"Where are you taking me?" Freddie asked.

"To see a doctor."

"Will he be annoyed?"

"Of course he will." I decided not to try and bamboozle the child. "Why did you do it, anyway?"

"'Cos Mummy locked me in. And I wanted to make me dad mad."

"But you might have been killed!"

"I wish I had."

"You do?"

"Yeah. So they'd lock him up again."

Freddie's father was no stranger to prison. His last sentence expired just a year ago. On paper, he is a male nurse earning less than eighteen thousand. His real *métier* lies elsewhere—he is an expert at handling stolen goods. He is also something of a fantasist and poet, but chiefly a crook. If only things were different in this country, he believes, he would be a prosperous businessman, but he is wrong: he would be a crook whatever the regime.

When he moved into the attic apartment after the pharmacist's wife was murdered four years ago, he came to see me, pretending he wanted to borrow a screwdriver. His dark eyes rested first on me, then on my books and furniture (he had no doubt made enquiries about me and come to the erroneous conclusion that I was a potential customer), and I was fascinated by those soft Jewish eyes, huge ears, and pugilsitic jaw. As might have been expected, he wore his hair brushed straight back and glistening with hair cream, and he gave off a strong scent of aftershave. If we still had old maids with dowries, I wouldn't need three guesses what his vocation would be.

There followed his introductory monologue, such as no self-respecting writer would invent and no actor perform, for in all art worthy of its name, one has to keep within certain bounds. I was to understand that he had been everywhere, knew everybody, and could procure or arrange just about anything. In the concentration camp he had shared a bunk with Count Schwarzenberg. He was on first-name terms with the Prime Minister's brother. He had once met Henry Ford while visiting Niagara. He was trying to obtain a set of silver platters for the Belgian delegate at the UN. He had rebuked the Deputy Interior Minister by saying: ''You needn't think you can pull the wool over *my* eyes, old boy, I can see right through you!'' When he visited Honza Schwarzenberg in Vienna the other day, he was introduced to Otto Hapsburg, a truly charming gentleman. An agent, of course. All those fine gentlemen were agents. Agents were in charge the world over—policemen of the world unite. Nixon and other clowns like him—he wouldn't even bother to name our ones—were just their lackeys. One of these days, when he had more time, he would tell me more about all this.

After ten minutes I was supposed to feel like a country cousin who has spent his life in total ignorance of the big world outside. After twenty, I might begin to hope that despite all his knowledge and wide experience he might consider me worthy of notice.

The whole performance lasted a full ninety minutes. During that time he managed to reveal how he earned his money—he would go to a second-hand shop and buy an ordinary carpet for eight hundred crowns, only of course it was no ordinary carpet but a rare Persian that had gone unrecognised, and he'd sell it for fifteen thousand—that he was having an expensive residence built in the university quarter, that he had an absolutely stupid but beautiful wife, two sons from his first marriage, a daughter from his second, and little Freddie with that absolutely stupid but beautiful third wife, that his second wife had been a doctor and had once treated the Shah of Persia, which he found amazing since his second wife, too, had been basically stupid, like all women, that his eldest son was such a stubborn bastard that when he had once tied him to a table leg, the boy bit into the table-top and hung on, so that they had to prise him away, and what a job that was, they had to throw water over him and that two-inch piece of wood (nobody had wanted to believe this) was bitten right through in five places. He also told me that he had been meant to study law but the war had intervened, that he had written two books, although he had never had the time to revise his manuscripts, but perhaps he could ask me to look at them sometime, not that he thought there was much money in writing (here followed the one and only, brief, pause in his monologue in case I wished to express an opinion on this), and he could get me a splendid set of silver cutlery that used to belong to the Kolowrat family, a pewter teapot, genuine Slavkov ware, several fine engravings, and a Louis XV commode.

Furthermore, he managed to describe his arrest in the fifties, which he glossed over with somewhat suspicious modesty so that all I could gather was that he had taken part in some kind of conspiracy together with Count Schwarzenberg and the war hero General Kutlvašr, who had flown with the RAF. I was not at all clear as to the aims of this conspiracy, nor did I attempt to find out.

I learned later from his wife (who was neither stupid nor beautiful) that he got himself arrested because, while acting as an instructor at a school for waitresses somewhere in the border regions, he had had sex with some of his underage pupils. This figured, except that I couldn't imagine how anyone in their right mind could have ever allowed him into a classroom as a teacher.

At the hospital we were seen by a very strict staff nurse. I explained that Freddie had fallen on to my terrace, or to be more precise, had flung himself on to it, possibly with suicidal intent.

"Are you his father?"

"No, just a neighbour."

She gave me a look which seemed to imply that in that case my part in the whole affair was highly suspicious.

"Does the child not *have* a father?"

"His father is at work," I explained.

"Can you give me his particulars?"

"I can try."

Between us, Freddie and I supplied most of the information required. Neither of us could give her his date of birth, but I promised to fill this in later. The nurse had an impressive bosom, and Freddie gazed at it with interest. And although I said to myself that I need feel no responsibility for him, I was filled with apprehension at what he might get up to.

Soon we were called into the examining room.

The doctor looked first at Freddie, then at me, finally again at the boy. He regarded Freddie with benevolence, me with a frown. "You the father?"

"No, a neighbour."

My reply quite obviously disgusted him, and he turned to Freddie again.

"So, young man, you jump out of windows, do you?"

"Yeah!" said Freddie proudly.

"And what would you like to be when you grow up?" asked the doctor, tapping the lad's forehead. "A paratrooper?"

"I'm gonna be a policeman," said Freddie.

"A policeman?" said the doctor, surprised. "Why a policeman?"

"So I can arrest me dad," explained Freddie.

The doctor gave me a dirty look, then realised that I was not the father, or if I was, Freddie did not acknowledge me as such, and he ordered Freddie to shut his eyes and walk five paces forward to the window and back again.

"I'd arrest everybody," mused Freddie with his eyes shut. "Grandad, granny, our teacher, *and* the cook at school."

"This child...," began the doctor, giving me a reproachful glance. "Oh!... Now, how did you fall, Freddie? On your hands?"

"I first went to the door and when it was shut," related Freddie enthusiastically, "I climbed up on the roof and jumped."

The doctor wrote out instructions for an X-ray and told me to come back when it was done.

We sat together in a gloomy waiting room, next to us a dying old woman huddled in a wheelchair. Freddie looked amused. He wanted to know where the wheelchair had its motor. Then he offered to tell me a story. It was a very confused story, about a kind stepmother and an ugly father who was a merchant and a cannibal. This wicked father-cannibal sent his sons out into the world to bring him the biggest pearl. Those who returned empty-handed he would fry and eat with onions.

I don't know if he invented the story himself or heard it from someone else, but that bit about the sons fried with onions sounded to me like something his perverted father might have dreamed up. But before he could continue, Freddie was summoned inside.

I cannot help thinking that I have been somewhat less than fair when describing his father. He certainly isn't as accomplished a villain as he would like to be. He lacks some of the attributes of the true professional, which must be counted in his favour, for to be amateurish is also to be human.

About a week after he moved into our house he invited me up to his apartment. He was wearing his Sunday best, his snow-white shirt equipped with a perfectly starched collar.

He had filled those two small attic rooms with old furniture, nothing of any particular value, but most of the stuff dated from the last century and people pay quite a lot of money for that these days. Just by the door in the hall, hanging in a totally unsuitable place, there was a large canvas with a Cubist painting of a nude.

"This here is a Picasso," he opened fire with his heaviest guns. "Unfortunately, it ain't signed."

"This is no Picasso," I stopped him in his tracks. "Never has been and I don't expect it ever will be."

This quelled him a little. "But... but just look at those arms and those thighs! Who else could've painted them, I ask you?"

"Anyone could," I said.

"But Professor Matějíček..."

"Mr Vejr," I said reproachfully, and he, without bothering to finish his sentence, drew me inside to show me his collection of precious stones. I protested that I knew nothing about precious stones, but that seemed only to encourage him. He took a canvas bag out of the escritoire, a bag such as ladies use to carry their suntan lotion and repellant cream to the beach, and shook out of it about a dozen small medicine bottles, taking out the corks and spilling the stones on the table. Here was a genuine South African twelve-carat diamond, while these two were artificial, this blue sapphire came from India, then he showed me three rubies, an opal, and two bottles full of Bohemian garnets. One bottle tipped over, the stones came tumbling out and fell to the floor, making a rustling sound as they piled on top of one another. He knelt to pick them up, and as he did so his jacket rode up his back and I could see that his shirt had been patched at the bottom with a large red-and-white checked strip of material.

Then he brought out his son's numismatic collection, all the coins neatly arranged in a thick album with a copperplate inscription on its cover:

Frederick Vejr—Coin Collection
To Freddie, on the day of his birth
from his Father

I was almost moved.

In the course of the first six months he came at least twice a month to offer me something. "Maestro, how about a super Baroque Christ? The carving's quite out of this world."

Reluctantly I went upstairs to look.

"But this is from the nineteenth century!"

"You really think so? Naw ... just look at the folds in that garment...."

But he did not insist any more, leading me instead to the sideboard, there to show me a wrought silver dish that used to belong to the Piccolominis—genuine ninth-century work.

Next time he turned up to offer me a real Hamadan. I had not the slightest idea what a Hamadan was, my expertise in carpets being about on a par with that in diamonds. The carpet had been stowed under the stairs on the ground floor, a huge roll, at least four times five metres. He undid the roll to allow me a glimpse of the carpet itself, garish colours covered with a layer of dirt.

"Well, what d'ya say?" His face glowed with enthusiasm.

"It's dreadfully filthy, isn't it," I said.

"Oh, well," he waved my objection aside, "if only you'd seen how they had stored the thing! But the craftsmanship! First half of the century." He didn't say which one, to be on the safe side after his experience with the Baroque Christ.

The following day I watched him as he dragged the Hamadan to the frame in the yard where the tenants beat their carpets. It was even larger than I had thought seeing it folded up under the stairs. Then he brought over a hose from the garden and began to spray the carpet with a mighty stream of water.

I stood on the terrace, watching him in amazement, which grew still further when I saw what was happening to the carpet.

I had never seen anything like it, nor had I read about anything of the sort. Together with the accumulation of muck, the colours started to wash away from the surface of the carpet, which turned white in front of my eyes while trickles of discoloured water snaked over the concrete down in the yard.

I believe that he too was stunned by the outcome of his cleansing operation, but having once started he didn't intend to give up. Then, right from the middle of the huge carpet, a piece of fabric dropped away; or rather, it didn't drop away, it dissolved and was no more.

When he finally turned off the water, a greyish-white rag with a gaping hole in the middle hung there in front of him. Mr Vejr looked up at me, threw up his hands, and hid inside the house.

Soon after this incident he bought a five-ton truck.

"What do you need a truck for?" I wanted to know.

"Oh, it'll come in handy," he replied. "And it was dirt cheap, too. Six thousand." Then he added: "And a little on the side, of course."

For two days people came and swarmed around the blue truck, while he kept putting its canvas top up and taking it down again and sitting importantly behind the wheel. Like a little kid. Since then—and it's over two years now—the vehicle has been standing outside the house, gradually losing the air in its tyres and its blue coat rusting.

Just a few months ago he bought a second-hand Morris— from the British Embassy, he said. For once, I suspect he was telling the truth, for who else in Prague would own an old Marina? The car was painted a light green and upholstered in yellow leather; it carried the British Leyland emblem.

"Dirt cheap, was it?" I enquired.

"A mere thirty thousand," he said proudly. "Try and get one for fifty, if you can!"

"I wouldn't. Try, I mean," I said truthfully. "I'd be worried about getting spare parts."

"Oh that! All I have to do is drop a line to old Alois in London and he'll send me whatever's needed."

I had no idea who old Alois might be, but I could appreciate that an enterprising trickster could use a Morris Marina. Silently he draws up outside the house of an old lady who has put an ad in the papers that she wants to sell a Baroque angel. He gets out of his light-green car, takes off his leather gloves, and holds out his hand to the old lady, introducing himself as Dr Vejr. He'll chatter on about the state of the world, about Renaissance sixteenth-century chests, about Gothic madonnas from the latter part of the fifteenth century, about Dr Vojtíšek and Professor Bruncvík and other famous art experts, and then, just by the way, drop a remark about his visit to Chagall. The old lady is quite carried away, and in the end it is left to him to fix the price. And he gives her three thousand less than a Baroque angel would merit. So far, so good, but there are just two snags: firstly, the Baroque angel will not be Baroque, which Mr Vejr won't even sniff, and secondly, if one is to alight from a light-green Morris Marina outside an old lady's house, this noble product of British Leyland has to be in working order. Mr Vejr's was—for just six weeks; then the gearbox went kaput.

Ever since, the green Marina has perched on its blocks beside the blue five-ton truck, the two of them rusting away quietly in unison. And old Alois still hasn't sent a new gearbox from London.

Freddie was brought back by a young nurse.

"Well, Freddie, shall we tell Daddy what's wrong with us? That we've broken our wrist and bruised our fingers?"

"I'm not his father."

"You're not his father?"

"No. I'm his neighbour."

She gave me a scathing look, as if to say I should be ashamed of myself for repudiating my own flesh and blood, even if he *was* illegitimate. Having obviously decided not to waste any words on me, she turned affectionately to the young policeman-to-be.

"Now, Freddie, you'll go along back to the doctor who gave you that piece of paper, won't you."

She thrust a metal rod into my hand with Freddie's X-rays threaded on it, and the two of us hurried back to the casualty department. As we sat down on the white bench in the waiting room I saw that the child, broken wrist and bruised fingers notwithstanding, was smiling, his face adorned with an expression denoting some inner joy. Unaware of my scrutiny, he was completely immersed in himself, his injured hand diving into one of his pockets every now and again, as if seeking something.

"What is it, Freddie?" I asked. "Is there anything you need?"

Freddie gave a start and shook his head silently, his hand still in his pocket.

"What have you got in that pocket?"

"Nothing!"

He hesitated for a moment, waging some inner struggle. Then he could resist no longer. "Look," he said, pulling a number of objects out of the pocket: a ballpoint, a pair of tweezers, a small ceramic dish, a tube of medicine.

"Where on earth did you get all this?"

"She had an apple there, too, but I hate apples," he announced.

The nurse received her property with a gracious nod. I could well imagine how she would hold forth at the earliest opportunity about the damage to a child's morals resulting from denial of paternity.

Then they led Freddie, now unburdened of contraband, away to have his wrist put in plaster.

His father had last been locked up in the period between the blue truck and the light-green Marina. They turned up one morning in two black Volgas, carried out a house search in the course of which they confiscated a number of antique objects, taking them away together with their owner. As there was no phone in their attic apartment (nor is there ever likely to be, seeing that it wasn't meant for human habitation), a terrified Mrs Vejr came running downstairs to us as soon as the police cars had gone, asking if she might use ours.

"Of course, go right ahead," I said. "But do be careful— my phone is most likely to be tapped."

She nodded, but the word obviously meant nothing to her because she proceeded to speak on the telephone using highly libellous expressions to describe those who had just departed. Fortunately, the bugging is at the moment being done unofficially and is intended to monitor *my* conversations and not those of my neighbours.

After that, Mrs Vejr would drop in to see me from time to time. Since her husband's arrest she had become more attractive to look at, having lost her habitual haunted expression. She would as a rule stand in the doorway of my study (she invariably declined to come in "so as not to disturb") and launch into a monologue. She was an animated speaker, shaking her head a great deal as she talked, her long, dyed hair dancing on her shoulders.

So it was that I regularly learned how her wily spouse was doing in his splendid isolation. Quite contrary to his habit, it appeared that he was keeping mum and had refused to confess to anything. His lawyer claimed that as long as he stuck it out, the police would have a hard time of it, as they had nothing on him. This surprised me quite a lot, and I think she found it equally astonishing.

At first I tended to placate her by saying that I was sure it would all turn out for the best and her husband would be home before she knew it, but then it dawned on me that far from placating her, I was giving her cause for worry. There was nothing she desired less than the speedy return of her lord and master.

"Oh, Gawd," she said in panic, "if he gets the feeling that he's put one over on them, he'll be more uppity than ever. As if he wasn't big-headed enough already..."

I learned that Mr Vejr was twenty-five years older than his

wife, a mangy kind of Casanova and a braggart, but he had managed to get her drunk and "well, *you* know how it is, I was silly and inexperienced, and I was afraid to have an abortion but couldn't tell me parents neither, like that I was going to have a bastard kid, you see. Anyway, they say a child without a father hasn't got a dog's chance in life, don't they? But what kind of a father is *he*, I ask you? If you only knew. He'll go a fortnight without so much as looking at the boy, and then all of a sudden he'll start playing the fool with him, tickling him, sometimes he tickles the lad such a lot that Freddie has a fit, goes all red in the face and can't catch his breath. And you should see what my old man gets up to with me...."

Next time she told me that her husband had arranged for his former associates, with whom he had sold all that junk, to give her ten thousand for household expenses. "Oh, they weren't very keen at all, you bet," the young woman narrated, shaking her head about as she spoke, "but he sent them a message from prison that he'd land them all in it if they didn't cough up. So they came round to see me last night, wanted me to write and tell him that I'd been well taken care of. But what I can't understand is how he can do all this when he's . . . well, you know, in the clink. Just imagine what he'll be like when they let him out, he'll think he's the master of all creation, so help me!"

"Oh, don't worry," I comforted her, "they won't let him out for a long time yet. I've never heard of anyone in our country whom they'd release just like that after six months in custody."

"You really think so?" she said, sounding hopeful all of a sudden. "Well, whatever, even if they do I can take it. I don't take any notice of his stupid jabber any more. But Freddie, that's something else again, he's too young to know what's what and he always listened to his father as if he was preaching the Gospel. And as soon as the old man went out he'd be imitating him. He'd sit at the table and yell at me: 'Now, Mother, bring me this, give me that!' And his language! You know what he called me once? A silly old cow, that's what he called me. 'You want a smack around the ear-hole, you silly old cow?' that's what he said when I didn't hand him his spoon that he'd dropped. A child of four and he talks to his mother like that—I ask you. And once he told me he'd have everybody locked up because everybody was bloody stupid, only he and his dad weren't. How's he going to end up? With his father home he'd only turn into a criminal too.''

The young woman dried her eyes. ''Now in the last six months he's a different child, so sweet, and never a nasty word. He even helps me do the housework. If only they'd keep his father where he is for at least three years more!'' That hopeful note sounded in her voice again. ''The lawyer says it really looks like it.''

Freddie's father spent eight months in custody before they brought him to trial.

That morning, she rang my bell. She was wearing a new two-piece, her hair was freshly permed, her hand moist as she shook mine. ''Keep your fingers crossed,'' she said in a tremulous voice, ''if only for Freddie's sake.''

Two days later the scoundrel was back home. Acquitted for lack of evidence. True, the prosecutor had lodged an appeal, but....

It was quite incredible. I asked around among my lawyer friends, but none of them could remember anything like it in the last five, maybe fifteen years. Here was a man in police custody for eight months and he gets sent home for lack of evidence. At the very least, my friends said, you would have expected them to give him a sentence equivalent to the time he had spent in custody. ''I hope you realise,'' one of the lawyers said to me, ''that if they released him like this, it wasn't for nothing. I don't necessarily mean to say that he's being asked to spy on *you*, maybe they just wanted to plant their own man among the fences. But once he starts working for them....''

The following week he showed up, offering me a precious

eighteenth-century vase. As if nothing had happened. I said I was not a china collector because it would not last long in my household. A week or so later and he was back with another suggestion: he had exhausted his financial reserves, apart from which, of course, he now had to watch his step, and so he had severed all connection with his former pals. Now I, he was sure, had some money to spare, while he had valuable experience and certain contacts. Why didn't we pool our resources—he could promise a twenty percent return within a month on every crown I invested.

It was so blatant that I thought it couldn't be a provocation. More likely his own initiative. I told him I'd make a bad partner as I was under police surveillance already.

He seemed surprised that the police could possibly take an interest in someone like me, who was not involved in the antique business. But he offered to ask Vendelín about my case, a friend of his who was now working as secretary to the Deputy Interior Minister.

The examination room door opened and the nurse came out.

"Could I speak to the boy's father, please," she said, addressing me.

I rose to my feet, and she beckoned me to follow her.

Freddie was sitting on a low white stool, his hand encased in plaster.

The doctor was so young and attractive I could hardly bear to look at her. "Mr Vejr," she said severely, "are you aware that your boy shows suicidal tendencies?"

I nodded, resigned now to my mistaken identity, and wondered how I could set about making a date with her. It was so tempting—not just her stunning looks but this unusual opportunity to sail under a foreign flag.

"You really must take him to see a psychiatrist," said the stunning young doctor. "Now, you have to understand that any delay is to be avoided, a specialist will be able to advise you on how to prevent a repetition of what happened. Surely you don't want it to happen again one of these days?"

She crossed over to me and said in a whisper, so that Freddie should not hear: "Your son's life is at stake. He's such a lovely boy. And so brave. He didn't bat an eyelid, whereas many an adult will scream and carry on when we're setting their bones."

She smelled of freshly laundered linen. If only I did not have in tow the wretched offspring of the incorrigible swindler who, God forgive him, was now most probably earning a little extra by picking up gossip about my private life, I would have told her now enchanting I found her, or I might even have asked if I could wait for her outside when she finished work. As it was, I only managed to say: "You can rely on me, Doctor. Freddie mustn't be allowed to perish, for I believe he's destined for great things." I had thought of saying "crimes" but decided against it in case she felt I was making fun of her.

When we had sat down in the car, Freddie looked at his huge hand with evident relish. "When I get home," he said, "I'll thump me dad with this. And then I'll throw 'im out the window."

"Now, Freddie," I said quickly, "I must ask you never again to throw anyone or anything on our terrace."

"No, not on the terrace," he said, as if to put my mind at rest. "I'll throw 'im out into the street. So he croaks."

"Why should you want to kill your father?"

"So he don't tickle me any more," he explained. "Nor me mum."

Mrs Vejr saw us coming from her window. She raced downstairs, shouting "Freddie!" Then, turning to me: "I found the door locked and the window open and blood on your terrace! What have you done, Freddie?"

"It's nothing, Mrs Vejr," I told her. "All's well."

"What *have* you done?" sobbed Mrs Vejr, not to be consoled. "I expect the poor boy got scared his father would be back before I was, but I *told* him I'd be back in a jiffy." She pressed Freddie to her bosom, crying all the time. "You know your Mummy loves you, your Mummy couldn't live without you. Why, I'd have to jump out of the window too if anything happened to you.''

I was looking at Freddie, clasped in her embrace, and to my surprise watched his face beginning to pucker up and tears starting to flow from his eyes.

He was crying at last.

TUESDAY MORNING

A Sentimental Story

On Tuesday, at about nine in the morning, the phone rang. I invariably answer by giving my name, but those who are calling me don't usually give theirs. It's understandable: the tappers who listen in to all my phone calls know full well who is speaking at *my* end, but they don't have to know who is at the other. Sometimes, though, it happens that I don't know either. This time the voice at the other end seemed quite unfamiliar. "Lída here. Forgive me, but could you tell me what your profession is?"

"My profession?"

"Yes, that's right, yours."

"Are you carrying out some research that you want to know this?"

"No, I just want to know if I've got the right man."

I seemed to detect a slight foreign accent. I hesitated for a moment, wondering whether I hadn't heard the voice before, after all. "Well, I have several professions. . . ."

"It *is* you, Mirek, I recognise your voice," she interrupted joyfully. "I'm here for two days and I'd like to see you."

"Where have you come from?" I asked, her voice suddenly seeming more familiar.

"Just now from London, but I live in New York."

"I see. Where are you calling from?"

"I'm in that hotel just round the corner from Wenceslas Square. In a narrow street. I think it's called the Alcron. All these hotels...I get them mixed up. You know which one I mean, don't you?"

I said I did.

"Can you come?"

"Now, this minute?"

"If it's not inconvenient."

"OK. I'll be there in an hour. What's your name these days?"

"I'll be waiting in the lobby. You won't have any trouble recognising me—everyone says I haven't changed a bit." She gave a hearty laugh like a real Prague girl, and then I really did know who she was. It must be at least twenty years since I saw her last.

I met her when I was in my second year at university, and I had by then had my first story or two published. Although a little younger than I, she had already been married over two years, or at least that's what she told me. Fortunately, I never saw her husband. Nor any member of her family. She never let on where she lived, and I did not try to find out. She worked in a small bookshop in suburban Vršovice. We locals knew it as Myšík's Bookshop, even though it had been nationalised some years previously and Mr. Myšík sent to work in the coal mines. But that is where I got to know her. I first went there to look at the books, then at her. I have almost forgotten what she looked like, just as I no longer remember what books I bought there. I think she had a fairly ordinary appearance, blue eyes, perfect teeth like Monica Vitti (whom I didn't know at that time, not even by name), and she wore golden earrings. I didn't like the earrings, but those blue eyes aroused my desire.

I felt I had to gain her confidence, somehow. Once, when we were alone in the shop, she went in the back room and brought me several books which had long ago disappeared from the shelves. They included Hemingway, Steinbeck and Maurois, an oasis in the parched desert of available reading matter. With those few books she doubtless did far more for my knowledge of modern literature than all my professors at the faculty, but at the time I was not yet able to appreciate that.

When I had browsed in that shop for perhaps the tenth time (by now I knew the titles of all the books on the shelves and on the counter by heart) I plucked up courage to ask her what she did after work. She replied that she hurried home to her husband, but then added that she was sometimes free at lunchtime.

Next day we spent the lunch break strolling in the nearby park, and again the day after. I don't of course remember what we talked about, but I am sure I must have tried to impress her with my literary triumphs, and undoubtedly I also preached to her about our new society, being at an age when one is still capable of enthusiasm for revolutionary ideals and violent change, and when that which fills wiser souls with horror or at least with dire foreboding is dismissed as mere teething troubles not worth worrying about. I wished to convince her that we were living in wonderfully exciting times, when the revolution had liberated working people and put an end to exploitation.

Had I but known it, I could have saved my breath because, unlike me, she had come to know our wonderful revolutionary times from the receiving end. Her parents had had their shop taken away from them, some of her relations had been imprisoned, and she herself was not allowed to study at the university. Some liberation!

In those days I also had pretty definite views on what a woman whom I might love should be like, and what rules were to be observed when falling in love. I was absolutely convinced that it was not the thing to do to fall in love with a married woman, for instance, so that had it been left up to me we should never have got beyond discussions on politics and literature.

We had known each other for about two weeks when she suggested that we take a walk in the direction of Bohdalec. She had two hours off for lunch, and this didn't seem enough for such a long walk, but she assured me I was wrong. We would get there in a quarter of an hour, she said.

At that time Bohdalec was still a wilderness on the edge of the city. On warm evenings it was doubtless the destination of many a courting couple who had nowhere else to go to lie in each other's arms. I had no idea that one could go there with the same intention at high noon. And, true enough, we got there in a mere twenty minutes. The place was deserted and silent as the grave, the silence only broken occasionally by the sound of a railway engine from the distant Vršovice depot.

From our high vantage point we could see the marshalling yards, and I remember to this day the sight of those railway lines gleaming in the sun, with the locomotives being shunted along them, looking unbelievably tiny at this distance. I was about to sit on a sunny slope and carry on pontificating about Maxim Gorky or the gradual withering away of the State, but my companion, with an assurance that betrayed a thorough knowledge of the local geography, led me further along the forest path, past a low barbed wire fence, all the way to a spot where the fence had been broken and where she indicated that I was to follow her into the fenced-in area. There, in a clearing so small that it felt as if we were in a ship's cabin, we lay in the grass and kissed and then, before I even had time to recall my moral principles, made love.

My initial reaction was one of shock at the enormity of what I had done, and perhaps even more at what *she* had done (after all, she was the married party). I fully expected a torrent of tears or reproaches, but she seemed quite calm, her face showing every sign of contentment, possibly even happiness.

I did not have a girl friend at the time and so I soon overcame any scruples I may have felt, letting my lust rather than my principles be my guide. Two days later we repeated the excursion to Bohdalec, and after that almost daily except when rain or the regular processes of the female body prevented it. Our relationship had but one purpose, or, in other words, it was monothematic.

We never met except at lunchtime, never went together anywhere else, neither to the cinema nor theatre, to an exhibition nor a restaurant. The streets through which we walked, or rather ran, were always the same, as was the spot which was our final destination. We called it our little room. And that's what it was. I cannot tell whether anyone else used it at other times of day. On a nearby building site I found a notice with the inscription

NO ENTRY
Trespassers will be prosecuted

I nailed this warning to a tree next to the broken section of the barbed wire fence, thus increasing the odds against our being discovered in our hiding place.

It was not exactly a comfortable little room, needless to say. No roof over our heads, no water, running or otherwise. We had no blanket or sheet. Only my raincoat, which I always, rain or shine, took with me, much to my mother's surprise, and spread out underneath us. While she started bringing along a large silk scarf with which to cover my nakedness (hers being covered by me), though at critical moments it invariably slipped off and revealed all.

We had exactly seventy-five minutes for our love-making. We talked in the intervals. But somehow it didn't seem appropriate to hold serious conversations about the meaning of life, and this eliminated me as an equal partner. And so I mostly listened to her brief accounts of what she had done the day before, what she had cooked for supper, how Joe, her husband, had again been nasty to her, how she visited her brother. For all this talk, she revealed next to nothing about her family or her past. Her deceased father had been a bookseller. She had some relatives living in America. They were very rich and she made out it was a foregone conclusion that one day she would pay them a visit and not come back. I learned nothing much about her husband, having no idea what he looked like or what he did for a living. Sometimes he cropped up in her conversation as an illiterate boor, sometimes as a gentle and cultured companion. He could have been an engineer, a mechanic, or an architect. If I asked her straight out, she would only laugh and say it was better for both of us if I didn't know. In the end I began to believe that her husband was engaged in some important official and therefore also secret work, and this lent the whole affair an exciting *frisson*.

On one occasion, she would tell me she had spent last night in the night club at Barrandov, where she saw a dozen famous film stars, or again that on Sunday they had driven down to South Bohemia at the invitation of a former industrialist who threw a grand dinner party. Which industrialist? It didn't matter, I wouldn't know him anyway. It could all have been true, but then again it probably wasn't. As if former industrialists were in a position to give grand dinner parties.

One day—and I was frequently to recall this particular conversation in the years to come—we did get on to a serious subject. She asked if I wouldn't prefer to live in another country. I couldn't understand why I should want to. Well, she said, if for instance someone I loved lived there? What if *she* were living there?

I said that she lived *here* and that I was glad she did, because I loved her and I loved this country. I went on at some length about one's fatherland and the culture in which one was born. She listened, or so I thought, with interest, even with some emotion. Later, at home, I tried to fathom what she might have meant by her question, and I was startled by a sudden premonition: her husband was a diplomat (that would explain the cloak of secrecy in which she enveloped him, as well as his contacts in high places and their participation in posh dinner parties), he was about to be posted abroad, and she would of course go with him. This prospect made me feel so sorry for myself that I could hardly sleep that night, and the next day I put several questions of my own to her which I considered extremely subtle, with the intention of discovering her husband's identity. She, however, saw through them and left me as unenlightened as ever.

That summer my parents and brother went away on holiday and I was on my own in the apartment. On the very first day I tried to persuade her to come to my place, extolling all the advantages of a real room as compared with our "little room" in the woods. She refused, saying someone might walk in unexpectedly. She felt safer in our usual spot. Also, there what we were doing didn't seem so much like adultery because she couldn't get used to me, nor was she "so aware of me". It seemed that to be aware of someone was more sinful where she was concerned than making love to them.

What about the evening? I wanted to spend at least one evening with her, to embrace her in the dark without having to hurry or look at my watch.

Oh no, in the evening she had to be with her husband. And so we continued our excursions to Bohdalec while my apartment stayed empty. Well, at least it was a nice, warm summer. Only once were we caught by a sudden shower, and I still remember the sensation of the unexpected rain licking my bare bottom, cold and wet. And once a small child disturbed our solitude. I heard a rustling in the grass and, raising my eyes from her face, saw the kid standing in the bushes just a few paces away. It could not have been more than five years old, and I could not make out if it was a boy or a girl. For a fleeting moment we stared at one another. I made a hasty attempt to cover myself with that ridiculous scrap of silk, but the child turned round and fled, crying loudly.

Only then did she open her eyes and look up. But all she

said was: Oh well, a small kid like that can't read—so the notice didn't help.

As the summer gave way to autumn, the weather turned very cold, and it rained all the time. I no sooner spread my raincoat on the ground than it was soaked through; also, I had to clean the mud off surreptitiously at night so that my mother wouldn't see. Our ''little room'' had come to the end of its usefulness. I visited her several times at the bookshop, buying books I didn't need and trying to lure her to the cinema, or at least to come and have lunch with me. She declined everything. The winter would pass, she said, and in the spring we would go back to our nook in the woods. I tried to get her to promise, afraid that she would forget all about me long before the spring. No, she kept repeating, I was not to worry, we would definitely meet again.

A few days later I came to the shop and she wasn't there. For a long time they wouldn't tell me what happened to her. Either they didn't know themselves, or they thought I was an *agent provocateur*. Then, at last, the new manager hinted that she had gone ''over the hill'', which was the term people used about someone who had fled the country.

I could not believe she had done it. It was as if she had died, and throughout the following spring I found myself frequently glancing anxiously at the barometer to see if it would be warm and dry enough by noon to lie on the ground in the woods.

A year or two later she sent me a postcard from the USA. The message was so impersonal that if she had not addressed me as ''Mirek'' I would not have been certain that it was from her. There was no return address, and in any case who knows if in those days I would have had the courage to write to her.

Now, at the Alcron Hotel, I of course *didn't* recognise her. Strangely enough, she recognised me. She rose from her leather armchair and came to meet me, smiling. She still had teeth like Monica Vitti, but instead of the earrings I had disliked she now wore large golden hoops; round her throat she had a golden choker. "Hi, Mirek," she said, and kissed me.

Her make-up was so flawless that you could not detect a single wrinkle on her face. She was, if anything, even more appealing than I had found her all those twenty years ago.

I sat down in the armchair opposite. There was a drink on the little table between us, and she asked if she could order one for me. But I couldn't drink as I had come by car, and anyway it was up to me to play the host.

"As you wish," she said, smiling again and looking at me intently. Or was it—I wondered—a provocative look she was giving me? She told me she was visiting Prague with her husband. He was here on business and had a very full schedule, so that she was free until late that evening.

"Not just at lunchtime, then?" I asked.

She smiled.

"And your husband . . . is it still the same one?"

"Same? What do you mean?"

"I mean Joe."

"Joe?" she asked, puzzled. Then recognition dawned. "Oh, him! I think I invented him, you know. Or did I? I just don't remember. My husband is American," she explained. "He's in the grain business—and beans and things. Terribly dull, but you get to travel a lot. And the money is good. I can visit Europe every year if I want to—or Australia for that matter."

"And you enjoy it?"

She shrugged. "Well, it beats selling books, I guess. Wouldn't you say?" And again she gave me that certain look. "But what about you? Are you married?"

I nodded.

"Any children?"

"Yes, I've got children."

"Two?"

"That's right."

"Boy and girl?"

"Here, you some kind of a clairvoyant? Or have you made enquiries about me?"

"*Everybody* has a wife and two kids," she said. "And half of them have a boy and a girl. How old are they?"

I gave two ages which weren't exactly right, but who cared?

"And tell me, are you unfaithful to your wife?"

"Of course not," I said.

"Of course you are. *All* men are unfaithful to their wives. And we to our husbands," she added. "You and I don't have to pretend, do we." She talked as if we had last seen each other only a week ago. Perhaps it was because she had already had a little to drink. Or maybe she had mastered the art of rapidly bridging the distance between herself and another person—at least in conversation. That is an art many American women excel at, preventing themselves from seeing that they never actually get close to anyone.

"How's life been treating you?" she asked, leaning toward me. "You haven't changed much, you know. Your hair is as thick as ever."

"Quite right," I agreed, "My hair's doing just fine."

"And you, how are *you* doing?"

"Fine," I said. "Like my hair."

My reaction confused her, and she changed tack.

"Such beautiful weather here. In London, it rained and rained. We spent two whole days cooped up in the hotel, just ventured out in the evening to see a musical. A dreadful show, somewhere in Piccadilly. You know London, of course?"

"Yes, I was there seven years ago. I even went to the theatre."

"You know what," she said, "I saw a play of yours once."

"Really?"

"At home, in New York. I kept an eye out for you, thinking you might be there for the first night. But you didn't show."

"No, it's a little out of the way for me."

"Maybe, but it would've been worth it."

"Also, I don't have a passport."

"You don't have a passport?" She did not understand.

"No, they took it away from me. Not just me, many people have had their passports taken away," I explained. "Writers, journalists, politicians, and so on. What was the play like?"

"In New York?"

"Yes, the one you saw."

"I liked it. A critic said it reminded him of Dürenmatt. You mean to say you can't leave here, you can't travel?"

"Well, I might be able to, but that would mean leaving for good. Then they just might let me."

"Well, why don't you?"

"I've already told you—I'm doing fine."

She shrugged. "You still believe all that nonsense you used to spout?"

"The answer to that question was in my play. Didn't you get it?"

"Yes, I got it. That's why I can't understand you."

"Well, we lead such interesting lives here," I said. "And a writer has to be a bit of an adventurer, you know. He gets bored if nothing much happens, conformity destroys him. Living here, I sometimes feel like a character in a thriller: cars with dimmed headlights, people tailing you wherever you go, searching your house. When I go to a friend's funeral, they even photograph me with concealed cameras, which aren't all that concealed, either."

"You *have* changed to some extent," she said.

"Have I?"

"You were always so terribly serious. In fact, you didn't talk so much as preach. You didn't seem to have the slightest sense of humour."

"Oh, that's just self-defence," I explained. "Against the absurdity in which we live."

She gave me a quizzical look, but as usual when I was

supposed to give a more detailed description of this absurdity, I felt a growing distaste which prevented me from explaining anything, complaining about anything.

We each of us have a few relatives and friends whom we are fond of and for whose well-being we fear. We go through life trying not to think too much about the inevitability of death. In this country, however, it is not only death that separates people, they're separated from one another while still alive by fear. And those who decide not to give way to it don't have an easy life. Some of them are driven into exile, just as Lída was two decades ago, and it is unlikely that I'll ever see them again, or if so, then not for many years. If we live that long. And what about those who remain behind?

I have a friend, somewhat younger than I, who during his student days was considered the great hope of Czech philosophy. Today, he is working as a night watchman. In the Institute of Philosophy. How about that for an example of our special kind of absurdity?

My former Chief Editor, a literary critic by training, has for seven years now been employed washing shop windows. Another friend, a well-known philosopher, is digging tunnels for the metro. The theatre director who dared put on my last play (last of those that could still be staged, that is) is serving a prison sentence; apparently he committed the crime of sending some scripts abroad. And so on and so on. . . . They have managed to silence the noblest and most creative spirits, raising the most spiritually impoverished and the most servile writers and philosophers. They have pulped tons of books, forbidden dozens of films; the censors have scoured the libraries, abolished news about the world and are doing their best to shut out foreign radio stations by jamming their broadcasts. They have bastardised the language to such an extent that it no longer resembles the language of our forebears. They have abolished churches, theatres, magazines, publishing houses, scientific societies and cultural associations—yes, they have even torn up the city's ancient cobblestones.

All this, and much else, is absurd enough—particularly when you consider that we have been at peace for several decades—and at the same time insignificant when compared with Siberian labour camps, mass executions in the aftermath of diverse revolutions, the gas chambers, or the Hiroshima bomb. And the real absurdity does not so much reside in the individual details I've recounted above, as in their duration, their agglomeration and daunting repetition, in the way they have managed to penetrate every nook and cranny of our daily life. In the end you become used to the absence of decent magazines and journals on the bookstalls, you get used to everyone everywhere celebrating some foreign revolution, you become accustomed and inured to all this so that you no longer take it in—but then one day, as you are about to catch a train, you wish to buy something to read on the journey and, after long deliberation, select a dog breeders' journal because you think that here at least there is a subject they can write about without humiliating you. So you open the *Canine News*, and there on the very first page you come across yet another wretched article about someone else's glorious revolution. This is when you get a fleeting glimpse of the utter nothingness which has you at its mercy; you as much as your dog. Trouble is, all this is incommunicable. Dante was wrong when he thought that the inferno and purgatory could be described. No, all you can hope to do is describe individual torments. That which is the most cruel about them—their endlessness —cannot be imagined but only experienced.

And so all I said was: ''You have a choice: either you set fire to yourself, or you make fun of it all.''

''The Czechs always prefer to make fun,'' she said.

''Not all of them.''

''Oh, I know, Czechs have also gone to the stake for their beliefs, or immolated themselves in protest. But hasn't it occurred to you that there is a third alternative?''

''What is that?'' I asked, even though I knew what she meant.

"Simply to get out."

"I guess I'd be homesick. Are *you* never homesick?"

"Sure I get homesick at times. Now and again we meet up with some other Czech exiles and reminisce about the golden city."

"And what about me? Do you ever think of me?"

"As you see. *And* that spot of ours. You know which spot I mean?"

I nodded.

"For some time we lived in Detroit, not far from the railway tracks. Whenever I heard an engine hoot I thought I was dreaming. Sometimes I do dream about that place. *You* don't even have to be there, not necessarily. I just dream about the wood, I'm lying there in the grass and looking up at the sky."

"There you are," I pointed out, "I have the advantage of being able to go there whenever I feel like it. If I feel nostalgic."

"*Have* you been there? Since that time?"

"No, why? You see, people only dream about places they *can't* visit. But I drive past there often. The wood is still there."

She leaned towards me then and said in a low voice: "How about us two going there? It's almost noon—it would be just like old times!"

I looked at that carefully made-up face, at the expensive dress which came from heaven knows which fashion house, and tried to imagine her lying down in the grass in the woods at Bohdalec. Still, it was *her* idea. . . .

Outside in the street a June sun shone in a cloudless sky.

"I'm so glad I found you," she declared as she sat down next to me in the car. "I have always wanted to go back there with you once more."

I turned round as we drove off, trying to spot the vehicle I knew must be tailing us.

"Who are you looking for?"

"Nobody."

She leaned across and kissed me. "Doesn't it worry you to be shadowed like that?"

"Not in the least," I said. "In other countries this sort of treatment is reserved for the most prominent people."

"But do you have to put up with it?"

"Yes, if I want to go on living here."

"And you do—you want to go on living here even though they treat you like dirt?"

"It's home, isn't it," I said wearily. "A man needs to belong some place. Does that make me an eccentric?"

A red Fiat had now been behind us across at least five intersections.

"Can you get into trouble for taking *me* out?"

"No, I shouldn't think so."

"Oh, good. I wouldn't like that. Do you mind if I take a swig?" She pulled a small flask out of her handbag and poured a shot into a tiny tumbler. She offered me one, but this was hardly the best place for it.

"I haven't told you how *I* live," she said, and started to fill me in on the details of her existence. Apart from their sumptuous New York apartment, she and her husband owned a whole island on Lake Michigan, where they had a luxurious home and two splendid stallions. They also had a house in Switzerland, and something in Hawaii. . . .

The red Fiat dropped away and we were now being followed by a white Volga. But then, there was always one car or another following you on a busy city street.

I asked her which countries she had visited, and she gave me a run-down of her travels on several continents. She must have spent a fortune and expended an incredible amount of energy, this girl with whom I used to make love in the woods at Bohdalec. Had she denied herself just a fraction of her extravagant way of life, the money she would have saved could have enabled one of my many former colleagues to live and carry on his calling instead of eking out an existence as a navvy. She might even have done it, but why, if she did decide to devote some of her wealth to charity, should she give it to a Czech intellectual? Why not send it instead to India and help feed a child who would otherwise die?

We crossed the old railway bridge and turned into a bumpy country road with small family houses strung out on either side. And then we were at our destination. She turned round in her seat, pointed to the back of the car, and said: "You've got a blanket back there. Aren't you going to take it along?"

I turned around now and saw that we were no longer being followed. Or, if we were, they had stopped before the last bend to keep out of sight.

"Should we?" I asked.

I reached out to pick up the blanket. How ridiculous, here in what was now a built-up area.

A man in a check shirt came striding past us, heading towards the wood, his hands in the pocket of his jeans.

I spent some time trying to fold the blanket so it would resemble a large handkerchief.

We were surrounded by high-rise apartment blocks, the once empty plain having been transformed into a building site. Two heavy trucks loaded with earth trundled along the rutted road that led past our wood.

"Tell me," she put the customary question, "what do you actually live on?"

"My foreign royalties."

We had reached the wood and were walking along our old path.

She looked quite out of place here, in her high-heeled shoes and her fine clothes in which only yesterday she had strolled along Oxford Street.

"Will you find the place?"

"I'll try."

From the building site behind us came the noise of a crane, and someone giving orders to the workers in a raucous voice. It occurred to me that perhaps this wasn't the right path, after all. Maybe they had felled some of the trees, and those that remained had grown out of all recognition.

"I can't understand why you insist on living here when you publish your books abroad."

"*Where* you publish isn't really so important," I told her. "Rather, what you write about."

"So, what *do* you write about?"

"About all this!" I said.

The barbed wire fence was of course no longer there, nor the warning notice. The bushes had gone, too. The wood was completely transparent now, we could see right to the other side, where several old-age pensioners were sitting on benches, enjoying the sun.

We turned back. "Maybe that wasn't the right path," she said. "Let's try to find another."

"All the paths are wrong. That spot doesn't exist any more."

"Come on, surely we aren't just going to give up!"

"You shouldn't have left."

"But I had to!"

"Why?"

"I just....I just couldn't live here." She stopped and stretched out her arms. We embraced and kissed. Someone was coming up the path behind us, the man in the check shirt and jeans, a professionally nonchalant look on his face.

"Have you ever thought of me?"

"I thought of you a lot that time when you disappeared."

"I wrote you several letters but never got a reply."

"I only had one card, that's all."

"Really?"

"That's nothing unusual," I explained. "They simply stop your correspondence."

We returned to the car.

"How about going back to my hotel?" she suggested. "My husband won't be back till late tonight."

"You sure?"

"He took a plane this morning. To Brno, I think."

"It's not exactly a good hotel for that kind of thing," I objected. "I'm afraid they keep an eye on all the guests. And the rooms are bugged."

"You're kidding!"

"I'm not, I assure you."

"But that's incredible!" She was again sitting next to me in the car. "Well, why don't we go to a different hotel," she said softy. "We can sign in under a false name, if you're scared."

"No, we can't," I corrected her. "Whichever hotel you go to, you have to leave your passport or identity card at the desk. They'll take down your name and send your particulars to the Security Police. It's not that I'm chicken, I just know the drill."

"Well," she said after a while, "you're not exactly the great adventurer you made out earlier, are you?"

How could I explain to her? I just said: "Look, we never used to go to a hotel in the old days, so what's the point now?"

She was silent.

"I'm sorry," I said. "Sorry we couldn't find the right place."

"Still, I'm glad you took me there, just the same," she said at last. "I'll remember our trip. You know, I guess I do get homesick sometimes. When I'm on my own at home. It's a huge house, twelve rooms. And I'm often alone, just me and my dog."

"No children?"

She shook her head. "The house can seem terribly empty, even though it's full of objects. My hsuband collects primitive art, and so we have walls full of masks and shields, embroidered skirts and totems. We have people in quite often, and then we talk about all sorts of things—about art and literature, and what they have seen on their travels. We drink beer out of cans, or gin, but then the next morning, when I wake up...well, you know how it is." She gestured with her hands, took a handkerchief out of her handbag and dried her eyes.

When we got back to the hotel I suggested: "How about having lunch together? Would you like that?"

"No, we never did that before either," she replied. "It wouldn't make any sense."

I agreed.

"I guess this is the last time we'll see each other," she said. "I'd like to ask you something, may I?"

"Sure, go ahead."

"You don't think you wouldn't be able to make a living abroad, do you?"

"No, I don't think that."

"Nor that you would be less free?"

"Hardly!"

"And you said you think they'd let you emigrate?"

"Yes, and I also told you why I didn't want to."

"Oh, come on, those weren't your *real* reasons. Can't you tell me why you really don't want to leave?"

I hesitated a little, then said: "No, I can't."

"Do you know yourself?"

I could have repeated that it was because this was my country. Because here I have several friends whom I need just as they need me. And because people here speak the same language as I do. Because I'd like to go on being a writer, and to be a writer means also to stick up for people whose fate is not a matter of indifference to me. At least to speak up for those who perhaps are less able to do so than I am, to give expression to their desire for freedom and a more dignified existence. All this I can do here, where I grew up, where I became part of whatever is happening and can therefore understand it, at least to some extent.

The freedom that exists out there, which I have played no part in creating, could hardly give me satisfaction or happiness, just as I couldn't hope to feel the sorrows of those people. I would feel that I was wasting my time. I could have said: Because I like to stroll over the cobblestones of one or two Prague streets whose very names remind me of the city's history, which I know and understand. But equally I could have said: My country is not to be found any more, it has vanished, just like that spot in the woods. Most of my friends have left, or are preparing to leave. The language I love is daily being violated by every means at *their* disposal—and they dispose of many and varied means. So all that remains is those few Prague streets. They have changed the names of most of them, and they'll probably change the rest before they're done, and they have let the city go to the dogs. They are even tearing up those cobblestones; rumour has it they're being sold for the construction of dykes in Holland.

It so happens that life often presents you only with a choice between two kinds of suffering, two forms of nothingness, two varieties of despair. All you can do is choose which you think will be the less unbearable, or even the more attractive, which will allow you to retain at least a modicum of pride or self-respect.

I could have given her so many reasons for and against, and still she would not have been able to understand. And so I preferred to reply by saying: "I don't know."

WEDNESDAY MORNING
A Christmas Conspiracy Tale

On Wednesday morning, the day before Christmas, I got up at a quarter past four. Although I had set the alarm for five o'clock, the thought of having to get up so damnably early had kept me awake since three. I shuffled off to the diningroom, which had a north-facing window, on whose frame was mounted a thermometer. Pointing my flashlight at the scale, I saw that it registered only a fraction above freezing. Cold enough for me not to relish the prospect of spending eight or nine hours out in the open, standing up and with my hands forever immersed in cold water. Still, it wasn't too bad for the time of year, so I should not really bewail my fate—it could have been much colder.

The kids were asleep, my wife too, and so I made my own breakfast and ate it in the kitchen. Then I put on two pullovers, a windcheater, and three pairs of socks. After yesterday's experience I would have preferred four, but my boots were too small for that.

I had been inveigled into this whole business by Peter, a former colleague of mine from the faculty. Peter was a lecturer in aesthetics, a literary critic and philologist. These past three years, however, he had been earning a living first as a night watchman in the warehouse of some building firm, and then as a stoker. During that time he had spent all his savings and, having discovered that it was impossible to keep body and soul together by honest toil, had decided to chuck it in and seek a more lucrative way of life.

I had not heard from him for at least half a year, and then he phoned me a week ago; after the usual questions about my health and work came a matter-of-fact query: "How would you like to sell fish?"

"How would I like *what* ... ?"

"Sell carp for Christmas," he explained. "You can earn a heap of money doing that."

"Oh but I..." The proposal was so unexpected that I completely missed my opportunity to refuse. "Well, I must say that's something I've never thought of doing."

"Of course you haven't," he said reassuringly. "Who would have? But you're a writer—you should try your hand at everything."

"I'm not the kind of writer who has to try everything," I countered.

"Sure you are!" he replied, his voice tinged with the authority of his former calling. "Anyway, you'll make a lot of money. You're not going to tell me you couldn't use it, now that Christmas is coming."

"But look, I've never killed a carp in my life. I just couldn't do it," I added, hoping that this would be the end of the matter.

"Oh, don't worry about that side of it," he said. "Leave *that* to me. And that apart, it's child's play. Two or three days, that's all, and you can expect to take home at least two thou."

An hour later he was at my apartment, to continue his enthusiastic depiction of the job he wanted me to undertake. Last year, one of his former students had sold carp outside the

White Swan department store, and in four days had earned ten thousand, tax-free. And even if we did not manage to get as good a venue—because that would obviously cost us— we'd still be sure to make two or three thousand at the very least. Of course, he explained, if we wanted a decent spot we would first have to grease somebody's palm.

At last I realised what he was after. He had a splendid idea, he was willing to put in some hard work himself and even to slaughter the carp, but he needed a partner with some capital.

"How much?" I asked him.

Peter had a squint. Now, too, each of his eyes was looking in a different direction. What I found suspicious was that neither was looking at me.

"Well . . . how much?"

"Say five hundred for the spot," he replied, "a hundred for the fish warden, and a bottle of brandy for the manager of the supermarket in front of which we'll do the selling."

"That's quite an investment," I pointed out.

"The more we put in, the more we'll make," he assured me. "And I've found a fantastic spot in Strašnice."

"What's that with the fish warden?"

He explained that if you wanted to make a profit you had to have decent fish. That former student of his—who had made enough money selling carp outside the White Swan to pay for a trip to India—had told him about some fellow who had ignored the fish warden. The fish warden had then simply called out, "Fish for Mr Scrooge!" and the soldiers opened a different tank, out of which came carp that looked more like minnows.

"Soldiers?" I asked, puzzled by this new element in the transaction. "*What* soldiers?"

"Why, those manning the fish tanks, of course," he replied somewhat uncertainly. "They tell me there are soldiers there. So what."

I did not share his confidence where the soldiers were concerned, but if the truth were told, it wasn't the eight hundred crowns he was asking that put me off. I simply did not fancy the idea of standing there in the street from morning till night next to a tank full of carp. In any case, I didn't particularly need the money, I had enough to live on and a little in the savings bank. Things being as they were I could hardly expect to be earning more. So I was not really interested in this extra cash, I wouldn't know what to do with it, unless I donated it to somebody. If you are willing to hand money out, you can never have enough. But for *that* purpose two thousand was a ridiculous amount.

True, a number of my friends were in jail, all of them dangerous subversives and conspirators, if you were to believe the indictment. That they should be cooling their heels in prison while we others were enjoying a degree of freedom which even allowed us to choose whether we wished to sell carp was all part of the Russian roulette that fate had been playing with us for some thirty years.

One of those in prison had been a colleague of mine in the editorial office of a literary magazine in the days when these were still being published in this country. Christmas would be just the right time to pay his wife a visit and bring her a little money.

I lent Peter that eight hundred. He left in high spirits, promising to see to everything, fish included.

At a quarter to five I was ready. I had washed, shaved, breakfasted, put on three pairs of socks and a pair of boots. Now I tried reading the sports page of yesterday's newspaper, but there is not much in the way of sports going on around Christmas, and we all know that there is nothing of interest in the rest of the paper at any time of year.

At five I emerged into the frosty morning. The thin mist smelled of smoke, sulphur, and bad humour. Soon we'll all choke and become extinct, just as we have poisoned the fish in most of our rivers. All we are left with are some bemused carp in a few select ponds.

Yesterday was our first day as fish salesmen. We reached

the agreed spot in complete darkness. The carp, which Peter had procured the day before, filled a huge tank standing in front of the dimly lit supermarket; its manager, a portly, greying, elegantly attired fellow, gave us a friendly greeting, his friendship having previously been secured with a bottle of brandy. He gave us a hand with the wooden counter we brought out of the storeroom, and then he dragged out an ancient-looking pair of scales. For a while he looked on, amused, as we attempted to align the scales on this complicated contraption, then he pushed us out of the way and, after making some fine adjustments, jovially assured us that it could now be relied on to give us five per cent extra per kilogram. He further instructed us never to fail throwing the fish on the scales with the maximum quantity of water—''tip the water out only if the customer has looked at the scales beforehand''—then snatch the carp away as soon as the indicator reaches the highest point, making sure at the same time that the scales should not ever show a whole, easily read weight such as one or one-and-a-half kilos. We listened most attentively, which encouraged him to give us some more useful hints. Naturally, it went without saying that we had to round the price up to the nearest whole number, if possible to the number nine, which was the best of all whole numbers. Then throw in a few odd pence on top, as that made it look more convincing. By way of example the manager thrust his hand in the tank, fished out a carp and threw it on to the recently adjusted scales. One kilogram nineteen crowns, then add a few pence for the sake of appearances—say, nineteen crowns sixty. Customers as a rule pay with a large denomination note and don't expect any small change. That gives us an acceptable price of twenty crowns. However, the manager continued our initiation with evident glee, it can happen that a somewhat absent-minded customer enables you to quote an even higher price, like twenty crowns twenty. In that case always demand your change back. If this proves difficult, you can show magnanimity by saying, ''Never mind, you keep the change—I'll collect

it next Christmas!'' Not only does that look good, the customer will usually demur and tip you a crown or two extra, *on
top* of the twenty. You can thus make three or four crowns on
a seventeen-crown carp, taking into account what you already
gained on the scales.

Noticing the astonished expression on my face, the manager obviously concluded that I was scared, and so he turned to
me and assured me there was nothing to be afraid of. Most of
the customers were women, who hardly ever noticed what the
weight was, much less were able to calculate the price. But of
course it was up to me to be skilful and to use psychology: to
sum up the customer, chat her up a bit so that she forgets she
is out shopping but feels she is making a date. And therefore,
men, beware of men! All this, the manager imparted to us
with a faint smile on his lips, as if he was not being serious but
just joking, merely playacting for our benefit.

''However, as soon as you mention the price you have to
be serious again. Sometimes it helps to apologise and say
you've got it wrong, correcting the price in the customer's
favour.''

He pointed to the scales, with the seventeen-crown carp
still writhing on top of them, giving us a graphic demonstra-
tion of what he had in mind. ''That'll be twenty-three sixty,
madam,'' he said, picking up the writhing fish and turning
towards me, carp in hand. ''Oh, I *beg* your pardon! Just one
moment, please.'' He threw the carp back on the scales, only to
snatch it off again, his face assuming so penitent an expression
that to harbour any doubt about the sincerity of his apology or
to defile that moment of truth by indulging in something as base
as addition or subtraction would have been to offend his integ-
rity as a salesman and his dignity as a human being.
''There,'' he cried, ''I almost cheated you, madam. It's only
twenty-two crowns ten.'' And with these words the manager
hurled the unfortunate carp back into the tank, packed with
its fellow-victims which kept opening their stupid mouths, as
Nature intended, oblivious to the coins clinking in their

throats for the sake of which they would shortly be fished out, slaughtered, fraudulently overpriced, and eventually eaten.

I got off the half-empty bus. It was only half-past five, which meant I had added an extra thirty minutes to the inevitable eight hours of freezing. The street was deserted, except for a few sleepy, obviously irritable pedestrians. From afar I could see our tank. The day before had not been a raging success, businesswise. Although women had trooped into the supermarket by the dozen, buying up everything from sugar to soap powder as if bereft of reason, to our dismay they appeared to be in no hurry to purchase their Christmas carp, perhaps because they had no room left in their bulging shopping bags; and so we froze outside the store for nothing. It was not till almost lunchtime that a few old-age pensioners and housewives took any interest in what we had to offer. I did the weighing and collected the money while Peter doubled as fisherman-murderer. He handed me the still seemingly live bodies, which I would cautiously place on the scales. The old ladies looked on trustingly, while the younger women exchanged a few sentences, some even flirted with me a little, so that I all but forgot that I was there to sell fish and not to make assignations. While engaged in all this chatter, I had my work cut out just converting grams into crowns—as for any rounding up, I lacked the necessary gall, cynicism and mental agility.

The women left and we were alone again. And cold. Peter started telling me all about Hašek's materialism and anarchism but then—doubtless influenced by the tankful of animal life at our side—quickly switched to animal symbolism in the works of Franz Kafka. He pointed out that with Kafka, man could always change into an animal, but never the other way round. In his view, the animal is invariably something repulsive, foul, slimy—a mouse, a mole, a monkey, even an insect. Peter could not say whether this included fish.

We carried on this conversation for a while, but it was too elevated a topic for those freezing conditions. We therefore played at being conspirators and succeeded (exactly how and by what means we did not for the moment specify) in forcing the government to obey our instructions. We ordered the immediate release of all political prisoners and restricted police powers to such a degree that they became practically nonexistent. We agreed that we would not put anyone on trial, and thus do away, once and for all, with the unending cycle of retribution which only created new victims. And finally, how else, we set about drawing up editorial programs—naturally consisting entirely of banned authors. We ended up with some eighty titles, whereas the total of carp we had managed to sell was eight. Not nearly so encouraging as the outcome of our conspiratorial activity.

At two o'clock we ''shut up shop'' for thirty minutes, adjourning for a hot cup of tea with rum to the storeroom at the rear of the supermarket. It was prepared for us on the manager's orders by one of the three young shop assistants who answered to the somewhat exotic name of Daniela. Her face, though, was typically Slav, her small nose flattened Russian-style, her hair probably a little reddish but you could not tell because she had recently had it dyed yellow, no doubt with a view to the approach of Christmas.

We sipped our tea, Miss Daniela sipping with us. Holding the mug in her tiny flippers, she looked quite delectable. She was generous with the rum, and so we felt very cosy with her in that storeroom at the rear of the shop. My friend, in keeping with his former vocation, recounted stories about famous writers while I, when asked to contribute to the entertainment, told them about my meeting with a former President. I don't think his name meant anything to the young lady from the supermarket, but she seemed quite thrilled to be rubbing shoulders with someone who had, in his turn, rubbed shoulders with a President. She kept eyeing me with what she no doubt considered provocative glances.

Arriving at our stall next day, the first thing I saw was the enormous pool of water licking the sides of the tank. I waded through it on tiptoe and, fearing the worst, looked inside.

Countless open fish mouths gaped at me from among the mass of carp bodies in that waterless container, some of the expiring bodies still twitching in their death throes.

I was seized with panic. There must have been a good eight thousand crowns' worth of fish in there. In all his calculations, Peter had never made any mention of the possibility of their total extinction. Quick as a flash I wondered if I had in any way been responsible for the catastrophe, but I could not think of anything I had done wrong or neglected to do. Then, stripping off my windcheater and rolling up the sleeves of both my pullovers—and doing my best to overcome my revulsion—I thrust my arm into the welter of twitching bodies. It did not take me long to locate the aperture through which the water had escaped, but it was at least another quarter of an hour (or so it seemed to me) before I found the plug. At last I did discover it under that mountain of fish and wedged it into the opening with all the strength I could muster. Any water that might still have remained in the tank would now no longer run out.

The trouble was, I had no means of filling the tank up again. Finding a paper cup in the waste bin I tried to scoop up some water from the pool on the pavement, but it was hopeless.

I threw away the cup and ran into the building that housed our supermarket. At this hour, naturally, it was closed. I crept past the doors of the apartments, trying to detect signs of life inside.

With the exception of the postman delivering a telegram, only *they* can ring a stranger's doorbell at six a.m. when they come to make an arrest. Only now did it occur to me that anyone in that line of work had to be quite shameless and thick-skinned.

I ran down to the cellar in the hope of finding a laundry room.

I did find a laundry room. From behind the locked door I could even hear a tap dripping. Taking my bunch of keys from my pocket I tried in vain to open the door. The thought of those dying carp lent me courage and I lunged at the door with my shoulder, kicking it several times for good measure.

The sound of footsteps up above startled me. I had enough to contend with already without being accused of hooliganism.

As I made my way backstairs I saw yellow-haired Daniela tripping towards the tank with a bucket of water in her hand. "These rotten tanks," she said by way of explanation. "Everything around here is rotten. Our freezers go on the blink at least once a month, usually on a Sunday. Come Monday morning we've got ice cream pastries and spinach running all over the floors. The burglar alarm goes off if somebody just *walks* past the shop window in the evening and it'll ring like mad, fit to wake the dead. Then the cops turn up and get the manager out of bed to check if anything's been taken."

We kept bringing bucketfuls of water to the tank, Daniela complaining all the while about the rotten supermarket where a person could not earn a penny on the side because all the goods came already packaged and weighed. Coffee was the only commodity you could make a *little* profit on, but for that you again had to have empty bags. She recalled her predecessor, who got hold of some Tuzex bags, which she filled with the coffee that was left under the grinder; she patiently filled the black Tuzex Special bags and took these all the way to Vršovice, where she sold them door-to-door, both for Czech crowns and for Tuzex coupons. With her coupons she bought genuine Scotch, which she then sold here at the store, making some two hundred crowns per bottle. In the end someone had ratted on her and she had to go, being posted to a pharmacy in Hostivař. Instead of coffee, she now had plaster-of-Paris to weigh, and instead of whisky she sold genuine South Bohemian wine.

By the time my friend and the cause of all my misfortune turned up, there was enough water in the tank for some of the fish bodies to turn their bellies heavenward and so demonstrate their pitiful demise.

We dumped all the corpses into a bucket, and as soon as the manager arrived went to ask him what to do with them so as not to infringe any hygiene regulations.

He glanced inside the bucket without the least sign of surprise, as if it had been he himself who had taken the plug out during the night. "How many?" he asked.

"Sixteen, I'd say," replied my friend. (Actually there were twenty, but I suppose Peter thought that by quoting a lower figure he would minimise our fiasco.)

"You'd *say*?" the manager repeated mockingly. "And now you'll want to throw them out, no doubt?"

"Well, what else?"

Astonishment at last showed in the manager's face. "What else? What *else*? Why, we'll gut them, cut them up into portions, and sell them at a higher price, of course."

And so I found myself in the warm and intimate atmosphere of the storeroom. With an apron, a butcher's knife, and the yellow-haired Daniela to help me, I stood over a much-used bench right at the back, hidden from the eyes of the world behind boxes full of sunflower oil bottles, to put the dead fish to good use.

It was a large storeroom, which smelled of spice and soap powder. In the corner opposite, a huge wooden crate with a hinged top attracted my attention. I had no idea what kind of merchandise it could be used for.

Miss Dana squeezed between me and the wall of boxes. Lightly brushing against my back with her breasts, she gave a delighted giggle and said wasn't it a scream to be given such a cushy job for a change.

I had never gutted a fish in my life, and so I watched attentively as her gentle fingers grasped the knife, cut open the grey body of the carp, and carefully extracted the innards.

"What do you do normally?" she asked. "Last Christmas we had a bunch of students here—but you're not a student, are you?"

"No, it's many years since *I* was a student."

"What you said yesterday about the President, remember? That was a lot of codswallop, wasn't it?"

"No."

"No?"

"No."

"Cross your heart?"

"No really!"

"Would you believe it!" She threw the portions of fish into a tin bowl. "What do they call you?"

"Ivan."

"That's not much of a name, is it?"

"Well, I suppose they didn't think so when they gave it to me."

"Not that I think much of *my* name," she admitted.

"What name would you prefer, then?"

"Lucia. Isn't that a lovely name? Lucia Masopustová," she replied in a dreamy voice.

"Otherwise you're happy?"

"What do you mean, otherwise?"

"With your lot."

The word "lot" seemed to amuse her. "Go on with you," she said, going over to the washbasin to rinse her hands. Then she pulled a chair across, sat down, and took a packet of cigarettes from her coat pocket. She offered me one, but I refused it, saying I didn't smoke. "Well, you can at least sit down, can't you." She took a wooden box down from the pile and placed it opposite her chair. "I don't have to tell you I'd much rather work in a greengrocer's or a gas station." She crossed her legs, shortening the distance between us. Although our legs did not touch, a mouse could not have squeezed through the space between them. It was obviously up to me to eliminate the space altogether. "Go on," I said. "Wouldn't you mind the fumes?"

"Mind? Have you any idea how much you can make in a month?"

"No," I confessed.

"Ten thousand, if it's a halfway decent pump. Eight at the very least."

"You're kidding," I said in disbelief. "Anyway, what would you do with all that money?"

"Lord Almighty!" she exclaimed, "You'd be surprised."

"All right, then why *don't* you work at a gas station?"

"Are you being funny?" She gave me a look full of contempt. Just then I heard a door squeak and then the voice of the manager. "Dana!" he shouted. "What's with those fish? Let's have some portions over here!"

Miss Daniela leapt from her chair, put out her cigarette, grabbed the tin bowl with six halves of carp, and made for the door.

I got up, picked up the next deceased and cut his belly open. I was itching to find out how Peter was doing outside, but I did not fancy leaving my warm haven. I would have to go out there before too long, though—it was hardly fair to leave a friend to freeze out in the street while I chatted up the shop assistant.

Daniela came back. "He says we'd better get a move on. There's a bunch of old ladies waiting."

"I'm doing all I can."

"That's all right," she said. "Fuck 'em."

And with this she resumed our previous conversation. "If it was that easy, everybody would be working at the gas stations. D'ya know how much I'd have to cough up? Twenty-five thousand at least—and *then* they'd put me in the storeroom for a year, where I'd earn bugger-all. And what if after that they give me the boot? Or if the boss whose palm I'd greased gets the elbow? I'd have to pay up all over again."

"So what about the greengrocer's?" I asked.

"It's all the same," she said dejectedly, cutting open another corpse. "You didn't get *here* for nothing, did you?"

She looked up at me.

"No, I didn't."

"What do you do for a living?"

"Guess!"

"How should I know. You're not a student, and you don't work with your hands. Maybe you've been in the jug?"

I shrugged.

"I see," she said, nodding to show she understood.

"What charge would you say?"

"Charge? You mean why they put you inside?"

"That's right."

"Black market?" she ventured.

"No."

"Embezzlement?"

"No."

"Or did you open your mouth in the pub and say something you shouldn't have?"

"Well . . . " I said noncommittally. I don't like telling lies.

"What did they give you?"

"Doesn't matter," I said, closing the subject with a wave of my hand.

"I know," she said. "My elder sister got two years hard labour. She used to work at a railway station. And she didn't do nothing, either. Just because she knew about the pilfering that went on. My dad did six years, but I don't remember nothing about that, I had only just been born. *He* did time because he had owned a shop. When he came out he said to us: 'I never stole a bean in my life, and let me tell you, I was a damned fool!' "

"What does your father do now?"

"He's retired," she said. "Before that he was in charge of a canteen. But he never learned the ropes. My parents just didn't know the score." She threw another gutted fish in the bowl and went on: "You know who *does* know the ropes? Him over there," she pointed toward the shop. "Our manager. F'r instance he used to transport the meat from the slaughterhouse in Budějovice. They always dropped off a quarter of the load for themselves and delivered the rest. But then the others got greedy and wanted to split it half and half.

Well, our boss knows better than that, he knows when it's better to call it a day. So he moved, while his chums carried on for another year, and then went mad and started buying houses and posh foreign cars and they all landed up behind bars. By that time our manager was here in Prague, delivering beer in cahoots with a guy at the brewery, but again he wouldn't dream of taking too much, he was too clever for that. Just a few cases from each truckload. But that was enough to give them each a hundred a day. And then he got fed up driving all the time and got the job here in the supermarket. He's been here five years now and d'ya think he's had a deficit in all that time? Not on your life!'' She raised her forefinger to emphasise the absence of a deficit under her boss's management. ''He's got everybody bribed up at head office, and so he always knows a week in advance when a stocktaking is due, so they can never catch him by surprise. *And* he keeps in with us, too,'' she concluded her eulogy.

''Want some more tea?'' she asked. ''I guess your friend might like some, too.''

On her way to the stove she again had to pass between me and the boxes that formed a high wall behind my back. I leaned backwards and felt her soft body trapped in the narrow space.

''Oh, Mr Ivan!'' I heard her protest softly. ''What're you up to?''

Now I suppose I should have turned swiftly and kissed her. But what then? And in any case my hands were covered in carp blood, and for some reason it seemed inappropriate to wipe them on my apron as a prelude to an amorous gambit. Before I could decide what to do, much less do it, I felt her moist girlish breath on my face and heard her whisper: ''Not now! If you want, I'll wait for you at six, when the shop shuts.''

At that moment we heard loud voices coming from the shop. They grew louder and louder. I quickly stepped forward, Daniela put the kettle down on the bench, and both of us ran into the supermarket.

There, between the shelves, stood an ugly wizened old man wearing ludicrously large, baggy trousers. In one white hand he held a metal cane, in the other a carp, his ruddy face aflame with fury. He was yelling at the top of his voice, and I gathered that he had bought a carp from us a little earlier and when he got home and weighed it had discovered that he had been cheated. By at least two crowns.

I was petrified, feeling as if I had just been caught out in some million-crown swindle.

The manager, on the other hand, was his usual calm, smiling self. He offered to weigh the fish again and exchange it for another or refund any money the old gentleman might have been overcharged, no one was infallible, but he could honestly not remember when they had last had any complaint of this nature. But the old man would not part with the *corpus delicti*, perhaps he was not even interested in getting his money back but just wanted to yell at us and make a scene. The manager— and I was amazed to find how much I admired his cool—took the old gent by the elbow and propelled him delicately past the check-outs and out of the shop, soft-soaping him all the time as he did so. He asked him to keep calm, urged him to take into account his, the manager's unblemished reputation, and again suggested that the customer have the carp reweighed, either here or elsewhere if he did not trust us.

''You're damned right, I don't trust you!'' shouted the old man. ''And I *will* get it weighed somewhere else.'' And with this he shuffled off.

Daniela's yellow head leaned closer to me and I again felt her breath as she explained that the crusty old man was Mr Vondráček, who weighed everything he brought home on his scales, even the content of tins, and then returned to raise hell in the shop. All the staff knew him and would usually give him more than he was entitled to but he never came back to *return* anything. Now of course he would go and have the carp weighed, but I wasn't to worry, the only scale he trusted anywhere in the vicinity was at the butcher's, and Mr Koňas, the butcher, would take care of it. Winking at me, she said that Mr Koňas had little magnetic bits of metal which, if need be, he would attach to the bottom of his scales where they could not be seen. When he took the meat off the scales he would unobtrusively remove the bits of metal so that the customer was no wiser and thought he was getting the proper weight.

Less than an hour later—I was by this time again out in the cold, weighing and wrapping up the carp we had resuscitated so that they could be murdered for profit—a broad-shouldered, red-cheeked man in a white apron turned up, and I was sure this had to be Mr Koňas the butcher. As he approached, Mr Koňas informed us at the top of his voice that we owed him a hefty carp. "You see lads," he exclaimed joyfully, "I weighed the fish for the old duffer and told him that you *had* made a mistake of twenty pence in the price—but in his favour! *And* I explained that a fish isn't a lump of cheese, that it loses weight fast as the water drains away from inside. He gaped at me just like a fish, his mouth wide open, and I bet you he won't bother you again for a month at least."

The butcher was still speaking when the manager hauled a plump, two-kilo carp out of the tank, killed it with a blow to the head with a heavy screwdriver, wrapped it up and handed it to Mr Koňas. And just then it came to me that in this world of ours there existed real conspirators, that there was a far-reaching conspiracy of those who had seen through the futility of all ideals and the deadly ambiguity of all human illusions, a resolute brotherhood of true materialists who knew that the only things that mattered were those you could hold in your hand or put in your pocket, that money could buy anything and that anyone could be bribed—except Death, which they preferred to ignore, and a few foolish individuals who could be locked up in prison, exiled out of the country or at the very least into subterranean boiler rooms, there to stoke furnaces and think their wayward thoughts. While I on the whole was one of the fools, at this moment I happened to be with the others, having been invited into their midst. Yes, now both Peter and I were one of *them*, enjoying their protection and solidarity. God help me, I almost wallowed in the warm feeling which comes of *belonging*. We carried on selling carp all that afternoon. More and more customers showed up, most of them women, until they formed a long line. The weather had turned a little warmer, and there was a touch of spring in the faint breeze. How much more pleasant it would have been out in the country, taking a long walk among the meadows—for me as well as for all these people waiting their turn in the line. But they had decided that they must have a carp, on top of the mountain of pork and beef and smoked meats, the potato salad, apple strudel, brawn and ice-cream and bowls full of Christmas sweetmeats they had baked these past few days.

I realised that I was beginning to hate this multitude, to despise all these people, and that this was the first part of my initiation into the general conspiracy.

Fortunately, at quarter past five we did away with our last victim. Then we had to clean the tank, put the wooden counter back in the storeroom, return the miraculous scales with our thanks, and count our takings. Peter took charge of the money while I went out again to sweep the pavement. And, since there was less litter than cash, I finished first. Going back to the storeroom, where that morning Daniela and I had cut up the dead carp, I sat down on a chair and closed my eyes. The air was warm and moist, the place was filled with assorted aromas, and hot water bubbled in the kettle. I reflected for a while longer about the general conspiracy. Not that I thought of it as some kind of Mafia; none, or at least certainly not the majority, of its members had any criminal intent, nor were they intentionally dishonest. They were, rather, ordinary, average people who had not been offered a single idea, a single worthwhile goal that would have given meaning to their life, and they themselves had not found the strength of character to discover them on their own. This is how a whole community of the defeated had come into being, bringing together a motley crew of butchers, greengrocers, Party secretaries and factory managers, bribed supervisors and coalmen and corrupt newpapermen and, no doubt, also those who had been appointed to uncover and smash this conspiracy.

My reverie was interrupted by the sound of soft footsteps, and looking up I saw the yellow-haired Miss Daniela, now without her white coat and dressed only in a blue skirt and white blouse. ''Mr Ivan,'' she whispered, ''do you still want to. . . . ?'' And she beckoned me to follow her, leading the way to the opposite corner where the big crate stood behind all those shelves. Seeing it at close quarters I noticed that it had handles on each side, like a cabin trunk. ''Here,'' whispered Daniela, lifting the lid of the mammoth coffin. Inside, I could see, everything was ready: blankets and two pillows.

Daniela quickly unbuttoned her blouse, while I made a start by hurriedly shedding my boots. Then we both squeezed into the crate. As I was lowering myself down next to her I saw that there was yet another handle on the inside of the lid, and I raised myself up again to pull it shut over us.

It was now almost completely dark inside the crate, just a gleam of light seeming to come from her yellow hair. Perhaps it was the peroxide—how should I know?

''Darling,'' I said emitting the customary sigh, and embraced her half-naked body.

''Be quiet, Mr Ivan,'' she whispered. ''You have to be quiet as a mouse, they'll be here in a minute.'' I felt her pushing my palms away from her body, then her flipper slipping inside my trousers.

''Mr Ivan,'' she whispered hotly. ''I saw straightaway you weren't just any old student come to earn a little pocket money before Christmas, and I didn't believe you'd been inside, neither. Your friend told me what you do, that you write plays for TV and earn heaps of money. Oh, Mr Ivan,'' she was by now agitating my penis with both hands, ''what's twenty thousand to you. I've saved up the rest and I know about a service station where we'd get it back in six months and anything we earned after that would be ours to keep.''

''You mean you want me to come in with you?'' I asked, astonished.

''I'll marry you and I'll be faithful to you for the rest of my life,'' whispered Miss Daniela passionately. ''That station is right by the highway, all the truck drivers use it and lots of those that go abroad, too. In a couple of years we'll make enough to buy a house, and you can have a brand new car and we'll go on holiday to the seaside. We'll have a marvellous life, what do you say?''

I heard someone calling my name outside, and, still bemused by Miss Daniela's loving touch, I quickly threw the lid open. Jumping on to the concrete floor, I ran outside to join Peter in my bare feet—or rather in my three pairs of woollen socks.

''I just don't understand how this could've happened,'' Peter said, standing there with several bundles of banknotes in his hand. He was so shocked that he failed to notice the disordered state of my attire.

''What's wrong?''

''That scale was fixed,'' Peter lamented, ''and we sold twenty carp in portions for almost twice their proper price, *and* you charged the customers the way the manager showed us.''

''Well, I did the best I could,'' I said, suddenly feeling that I had to stand up for myself. ''Did we make a loss?''

He nodded but did not reply.

''How much?''

''Eight hundred.''

''You mean we've lost what we put in?''

He shook his head. ''No, over and above that.'' He looked as if he were about to burst into tears.

''Oh, to hell with it,'' I said. ''To hell with all the money.''

The savings banks would still be open tomorrow morning. I would take out two thousand and take it to the wife of my colleague who was locked up because he refused to join the great conspiracy.

"I just can't understand how it could've happened," said Peter plaintively. "All those fish, and we must've made at least two crowns on each one of them."

I shrugged. In my mind's eye I could see all those conspirators, stealthily advancing on our fish tank under cover of the frosty night: our manager leading the way, followed by Mr Koňas the butcher and the yellow-haired Daniela and all the greengrocers and Party secretaries, factory managers and bribed supervisors, coal merchants and corrupt newspapermen.... Each and every one of them thrusting greedy hands into our tank and scuttling away with our carp....

"All I can say is that next time you want to sell carp you'd better spend the night with them."

"You think so?" His eyes seemed to light up as he got the message, but all he did was shrug his shoulders.

Well, I guess he was right, at that. It would have been no use. *They* would always find a way to cheat us, we just didn't belong.

THURSDAY MORNING

An Erotic Tale

It was actually a dead-end street, its pot-holed roadway leading only to the yard of a locksmith's workshop. A faded notice on a rickety wooden fence warned all comers that

TRESPASSERS WILL BE PROSECUTED!

But, since the little bridge over the evil-smelling brook took one right across the locksmith's yard, no one heeded the warning.

I, however, had business here and so could ignore the notice with a clear conscience.

I had come to see Mr Holý. I'd never laid eyes on him in my life before, but the water pump in my car had given up the ghost and I could not get a replacement for love or money. I had phoned every garage and every spare parts dealer in town, finally extending my quest to regional suppliers. I even tried bribing several managers—all in vain. In the end someone advised me to "try Mr Holý". At this address. Maybe he would deign to make me a new pump, steal one, or have one imported for me from Vienna. I had no idea why or how Mr Holý might be able to succeed where all the others had failed.

I discovered the workshop entrance at the very far end of the yard. A modest-sized hall housed a number of ageing drills and cutters—a more experienced eye than mine would doubtless have detected still other types of machinery. Standing by one of the machines, a yellow-haired man of indeterminate age was shaping a chunk of metal.

I uttered a greeting, and he looked in the general direction of the entrance, but I could catch neither a sound nor his fleeting glance. His eyes swerved to the side and fixed on the wall. There, I saw a dark opening which I supposed had once been concealed by a door.

Glancing that way I could see the end of a low bench, and on it two pairs of thrashing legs. One of these—quite evidently female—had its toes painted in dark red, while the other—in all probability male—was modestly attired in a pair of green socks.

"Good morning," I repeated my greeting, trying at the same time to gain a better view by taking a couple of quick steps sideways. Nobody was paying any attention to me. Over and above the whine of the processed metal I now quite distinctly heard loud moans and groans, about whose origin I could not entertain the slightest doubt.

I waited. Life has taught me to be patient, apart from which I invariably turn shy when brought into contact with strangers, particularly if I need them to do me a favour.

I sidled slightly more to the right, but feeling ashamed to keep staring in that one direction, forced myself to gaze, at least for a moment, at the opposite wall. This was graced by a number of posters extolling the exquisite lines of the Volkswagen and of a young lady who was leaning against the depicted vehicle. Then there was a scattering of portraits of other young ladies, in various stages of undress. The whole place gave off a somewhat lewd air.

I had put off my journey here for more than a week. My car

does not get much use as I, to tell the honest truth, am not overly fond of it. Not that I'm scared of driving at speed the way my wife is, but it somehow seems a sacrilege to send this mass of metal hurtling along the road purely on my account.

Now I could no longer see the legs on the bench in the next room. Instead, a dishevelled, golden-dyed head appeared in the dark opening. Briefly, it disappeared again; I heard a smacking sound, and someone gave a loud yelp. Then, over the screech of the machined metal, came a woman's joyous squeal. The woman now emerged in her entirety, blue clogs covering her red toe-nails, her body at least partly veiled by a white coat done up by its middle two buttons. She was thirty, if not a little more. Heading towards the man who had all this time carried on working at his machine, she asked: "You waiting for somebody?" without so much as looking at me. As she stood there she slipped off the right clog and used her big toe to scratch the calf of her left leg, this action causing her coat to open alarmingly. "Yes," I said quickly, "I'm waiting for Mr Holý."

"Not 'ere yet," she said, glancing at the man working on the piece of metal.

"Have you any idea when he *might* be here?"

"I guess he'll come." And with that she went on her way. As she passed him, the man lifted his hand and playfully slapped her bottom.

The woman gave another squeal, then said contentedly: "My, but you do have an adolescent mind, don't you, Mr Kobza!" As she spoke she looked straight at me, her eyes still smouldering with the blissful memory of her recent coitus. "Would you believe it?" she said. "He does that every blessed time I get anywhere near him."

She went out of the workshop. The man, whose name I now knew was Kobza but didn't know whether or not he was a mute, laid the finished component aside and picked up another chunk of metal. Mr Holý was heaven knows where, so there seemed little point in my loitering any longer.

As I left, it occurred to me to wonder where the owner of the green socks had got to. Could they be concealing Mr Holý from me? No, I thought, surely Mr Holý must owe his reputation to quite a different sort of activity from that favoured by the man in the green socks. It was to be supposed that Mr Holý spent this part of the day on the trail of various unobtainable spare parts.

A steep slope thickly overgrown with bushes ran the length of the workshop on one side, between the rickety wooden fence and the last of the high-rise apartment blocks. On the other was a scrap yard, separated from the locksmith's only by a low white fence. A narrow, deserted lane gave onto a street opposite the apartment block, a municipal water cart parked at its end. It showed the street its massive backside, which had been freshly painted a vivid orange. In this slowly disintegrating corner of the city, the water cart was, it seemed to me, the only object fashioned by man. I squatted on the grass right next to the fence, moved by the sight of this place. The smoke-stained façades, several factory chimneys peeping out behind the nearest roofs, and close by the railway sidings, from which came the familiar clatter of shunted waggons—all this brought back memories of my early childhood. We had lived on the slope above Vysočany, the railway line running right underneath our windows, with chimneys towering above it, chimneys which in those distant days I had found very splendid. My father, who believed in precision and factuality, tried to tell me which chimney belonged to which factory. As evening fell, people used to bring chairs and stools out onto the pavement in front of their houses and started to tell each other stories.

At half past eight a truck rumbled this way, shedding its load of tin cans in front of the scrap yard. The cans were not, strange to say, either rusty or painted, nor were they crumpled. It could be said that they alone could compete with the water cart in their glittering newness.

No sooner had the truck gone than the scrap yard gate

opened, and I was afforded another glimpse of the golden-dyed head.

The woman squinted at the sun behind my back, then stared at the pile of virgin cans. Advancing in my direction, she gave me a look in which there smouldered the joyous anticipation of another coupling, and said: "Ever seen anything like it?"

I shook my head, and she went back inside to fetch a broom, with which she proceeded to sweep some of the tin cans into the yard before hesitating in the gateway as if to see if I was going to follow her. Then she gave her dyed curls a shake, backed inside, and slammed the gate shut.

From the other end of the street a white-haired old man came pedalling towards me on a bicycle, his voluminous beard flowing by his side. He pedalled hard to gain the top of the rise, then jumped off in front of me. "You waiting for someone?" he asked.

He was wearing a vividly purple sweater and rust-coloured plus fours. My father had worn a pair just like those when he was about my age.

It occurred to me, quite without any foundation, that this might be Mr Holý himself, and so I injected a slight question mark into my voice as I said: "I'm waiting for Mr Holý."

"Oh, him," said the old man. "He doesn't come in much before noon, the scoundrel."

He propped his bike against the scrap yard fence, smoothed his creased plus fours, brushed aside his flowing beard, and loosened the knot of the scarf around his neck. The scarf was red with black dots, like a ladybird. Then he came towards me, holding out his hand and introducing himself: "Private Doctor of Philosophy Hovorka."

I don't much care for the formalities of introduction, apart from which the old man, while arousing my interest, did not inspire confidence. I therefore murmured my own name in such a way that he could pick out whatever his ear made of the jumbled sounds.

He did. "Pleased to meet you, Mr Kozina," he said,

ascribing to me the name of an eighteenth-century West Bohemian rebel leader, one of the most famous in all Czech history. "Forgive my curiosity, but are you by any chance related?"

I nodded. "Yes," I said, "an ancestor of mine."

"*Very* pleased to meet you," he repeated. "And what do you make of it all?" Fortunately he didn't pause to hear my views. "Just look around," he exhorted me. "What do you see? You see nothing but houses, chimneys, motorcars, grime, and stark eroticism. Whereas I, Mr Kozina, remember meadows, trees, horses, dewdrops, and the gentle embraces of young lovers. Right here," he pointed to the locksmith's yard, "there used to run a brook with water you could drink! Now," he went on, stealing a surreptitious glance at the closed gate of the scrap yard, "far be it from me to deny that I also remember grinding poverty in this neighbourhood. But the way the men who lead the world's empires have chosen to deal with it can only lead to disaster. I see you're surprised to hear me speak of men—yet you could hardly have failed to notice my conviction that all this world's affairs result from the conflict between the male and the female principle. And while in certain periods and geographical areas the love-filled and self-sacrificing female principle may have exceptionally gained the ascendancy, as is the case in Indian culture, the world was for many long centuries governed by a beneficial equilibrium between the two. Alas, Mr Kozina, in our own time, as you must be only too painfully aware, it is the male principle that has been triumphant. And not only is this inherently one that is bent on conquest, it also, as indeed everything that is male, has only a brief moment of usefulness, being otherwise superfluous and useless and, what is more, destructive.

"Kindly take one more look around you. And what do you see? Nothing but phallic symbols!" He raised a large, you might say symbolic, forefinger and used it to stab the air in front of my eyes, and as I looked I really saw the erect phalluses of factory chimneys, TV aerials, lightning-conductors, and cooling towers, monstrously bloated water carts about to penetrate defenceless hydrants, and I could not help noticing the obscene penis of a metal pipe sticking out behind the scrap yard fence. ''Yes, my young friend, you will see the sorry symbols of vanity and superfluity, which can never find satisfaction.

''The male principle despairs of fulfillment,'' the old man continued his lecture, ''and thus, like the Flying Dutchman or the Wandering Jew, it roams the universe, attempting to flee its own self. In its desperate attempts to escape, it has created the world of the spirit and of matter. It has discovered the joys of meditation. But all in vain!'' cried the old man. ''Every time, and in its purest incarnation, it invariably returns to its original mission, its one and only real ecstasy as provided by the winged Eros!'' He gave a strange, almost joyous laugh, his eyes resting briefly and with evident pleasure on the closed gates of the scrap yard.

''Please, do go on looking,'' he reprimanded me, pointing his symbolic forefinger in the direction of the four phalluses of the Holešovice power station, giving off mighty clouds of smoke. ''I expect you rejoice when, of an evening, the street lights come on outside your window, and perhaps you approve of the comfortable way you were able to arrive here on the municipal tram, but let me ask you this: *Why* did you arrive here? Why are you here at all?'' Now he prodded my chest with the symbolic finger. And all I could respond with was a feeble ''I don't know.''

''Right!'' he exclaimed, somewhat to my surprise. ''Quite right. There is no point to your being here. Last month, young man, I had to undertake the long journey to Mohelnice to visit my sick father. For the first time in thirty years I entered a railway carriage, and as soon as I started chatting to my fellow travellers I learned that they were all on the move for the most trifling of reasons. Superfluous motion, that's the watchword of our times. Last Sunday I walked up to Hradčany Castle and counted: eighty-two buses, one thousand six hundred and thirty-three motorcars—I did not bother to note the trams. However, thirty-nine thousand people passed through the castle gate, some having flown here all the way from America! And for what, Mr Kozina? They'll see nothing, anyway. It would be just the same if they were set down in Madrid or Kutná Hora, they wouldn't know the difference. It is for this that the resources which our earth has taken billions of years to accumulate are being squandered. These are criminal times we live in, young man, and before we know it our grandchildren will again find themselves living in caves, hungry and cold. Take this morning. I am retired now, but even when I wasn't, I always used this to travel,'' he said, stroking the handlebars of his bicycle. ''Just look at those multitudes rushing hither and thither on their way to work. Mr Kozina, all that noise and stench in the infernal morning half-light full of noxious fumes! And, what is more, everything they produce is pretty well useless. Either it gets thrown out almost as soon as it is made, or the scoundrels stuff their homes with it, where it only takes up room. I don't have to tell you, people put down a carpet, and then scatter rugs on top of the carpet, a fur on top of the rugs, and a degenerate lapdog on top of that. They cram books and paperbacks on to their bookshelves and never open a single one, and stand vases on top of the bookcase without it dawning on them that they were designed to hold flowers. Every corner they'll fill with TV sets and transistors and telephones and tape recorders. Wardrobes overflowing with clothes, these days, Mr Kozina, it isn't just the women but the men too who dress up to the nines, buying narrow trousers one year and wide ones the next and then the entire nation goes stark staring mad and everyone from eight to eighty starts dressing up like American cowboys. And when they fill one wardrobe they go out and buy another, and they build shelves to accommodate all their paraphernalia, their sprays and their aerosols, their pots and bottles of all the different poisons they put in their food and drink. Then you get people who install inflatable swimming pools in their homes, and fireplaces that work on electricity, and miniature fountains! On their walls they hang swords and sabres, whereas in real life they have never so much as held a garden rake in their hands, much less a lethal weapon; no, they kill with a fountain pen! And they use medals to decorate their walls, medals from battles they know nothing about. And then, when all this junk starts falling from their windows they go and buy a family house. For the sake of all that junk, Mr Kozina, not for the family! And then they acquire a cottage in the country, or an old mill. And every weekend, instead of turning their minds to something more elevated, instead of taking time off to think, they hasten to their cottage to clean and to dust and to make sure no one has stolen any of their useless possessions. They pretend that they're going in search of fresh air, water, and unspoilt nature, and yet every time they drive out there they contaminate the air we all have to breathe with still more poison until in the end we shall all perish.''

''Your father is still alive, then?'' I asked, hoping to provide him with an opportunity to calm down a little.

''Yes, he is,'' the old man replied. ''He's fine again now, he just had a bit too much to eat when my uncle killed a pig. My father will be ninety-five this year. And, do you know, all his life he has never once sat in a motorcar, and he only travelled by train when his unit was sent off during the First World War, and then again to the Sokol Festival in 1938 because he has always been a great gymnast. I followed in his footsteps, but when they abolished the Sokol I took up yoga instead. How old would you say I was?''

''Sixty?'' I hazarded a guess.

''Seventy-three,'' he said. ''I haven't tasted meat since I was twenty-five, and I was thirty-eight when I ate my last egg.''

''Were you a teacher before you retired?''

''I tried my hand at many a profession,'' he replied. ''I gave talks on vegetarianism to Slovaks from Rumania; I worked as a tutor in some of the most prominent families; and

I also did some Polar exploration. But as soon as I had made a little money, I always dropped everything and carried on my vocation as a private philosopher. Like Socrates, I strolled in the marketplace and addressed the people. And do you know how old this is?'' He pointed to his bicycle.

Before I could even venture an opinion he said: ''Forty-four years. Often I'll get on it in the morning to think and meditate, and I pedal away not noticing where I am or what time it is. I don't eat and I don't drink, and then it'll get dark and I'll look up and say to myself, ''I'm in Třebíč!' And so I'll turn up my collar and lie down under a bush in the woods and hope that I'll spot a new star in the sky.

''But sometimes these days it gets a little too much for me. Like the other day, I was just cycling down this very street when I suddenly felt so faint that I could hardly hang on to the handlebars. Luckily, the gate over there opened,'' and he pointed at the scrap yard gate, where a few glittering new tin cans were still lying on the cobbles, ''and I went in and came to a halt against a pile of waste paper. I fell off the bicycle and lost consciousness. When I came to, I was lying completely naked on a wooden bench. A naked angel was sitting next to me, and I heard music as if a whole choir of angels were singing. On the whole, though, I can't complain, I'm still pretty fit and can hold this position, which is called *salamba shirsasana*, for a full fifteen minutes.'' He demonstrated the position by standing on his head on the very edge of the grassy slope. And as he stood there, his legs pointing skywards, I saw his eyes fixed on the closed gate of the scrap yard. As if his gaze possessed some magic force, the gate opened and the golden-dyed head again shone in the rays of the rising sun.

The old man trembled, waved his legs about, and briskly resumed his normal position. Taking a folded piece of paper from his pocket he handed it to me with the words: ''A present for you, my young friend.'' And while I was busy unthinkingly stuffing the paper into my pocket, he hopped onto his bike and streaked past the white-coated woman in the gateway. I caught a last glimpse of him propping his bicycle against the fence in the yard, and then the gate closed behind him.

At that very moment, as if propelled by an unseen stage-manager, a little man in a leather jacket and corduroy trousers, his gait befitting a sailor or a jockey rather than the driver of a municipal water cart, crossed the road and made for his gleaming vehicle. His hands sunk deep inside his trouser pockets, he stopped in front of the machine and seemed to hesitate. The day was bright and fresh, and the street—except for me—completely empty. But then he overcame his reluctance, took one hand out of his pocket, and opened the door of the driver's cab.

The loud roar of an ancient two-stroke engine heralded the approach of an Aero sports car, poppy red in colour. Just as it reached the spot which could hardly be called a crossroads, if anything then perhaps the chance meeting point of two deserted little streets, the water cart backed up. There came the sound of metal meeting metal, but only for a second, because then the tiny sports car—that embodiment of the female principle of martyrdom—was cast aside like a discarded mistress. Its brakes squealing pitifully, it came to a halt in the middle of the roadway.

A very tall man in overalls clambered out of the low-slung little car. Leaning over the wounded rear of his vehicle, he paused in contemplation before wrenching off a piece of the mudguard. He raised it high in the air and emitted a sound like the baying of a very angry wolf.

A head poked out of the driver's cab of the water cart, then the man in the corduroys carefully descended to the ground, walked around to the rear of his gleaming machine, and only then decided to take his other hand out of his pocket in order to run it gently over the metal, now disfigured with poppy-red paint, and to test the water-spraying attachment. His direst fears were confirmed, for the attachment proved to be unattached on one side.

The tall man approached him slowly, holding aloft the warped piece of coachwork he had just wrenched from the maimed body of his car. ''You blind adventurer,'' he addressed the other man unkindly, ''you bumpkin, why the hell don't you get someone to keep an eye out for you, since you're purblind yourself?''

The corduroy-clad driver was sadly gazing at the spraying gear. No doubt remembering how gracefully it had squirted the water to every side while now it was disdainfully peeing on the vehicle in his charge, he muttered darkly: ''Oh, go and take a running jump, you stupid sod!''

Two old men came walking down the street. The first carried a string bag with several empty bottles in it. ''Look,'' he was saying to his companion, ''don't complain to me about it, go and tell the cooperative!'' He did not even look at the other man but was watching the two drivers with great interest.

''But the cooperative has already approved it,'' said the other old man in a plaintive voice.

The man with the string bag had a large, officious mouth and bushy eyebrows, which lent him a determined look, and the massive body of a wrestler, while the other, with his hunched shoulders, grey, sunken cheeks, and ears that stuck out from his hairless skull, had grown used to his role of the ever-complaining victim.

''They have been there three times now, men and women together,'' he lamented.

''Well, it's the cooperative's business. Let them decide,'' said the other, looking as if he was about to intervene in the drivers' dispute.

''And when they finish their exercises, they get up to things . . .''

The man with the officious mouth suddenly took an interest. ''Things? What kind of things?''

''First, they drag mats into all four corners of the gym,'' the other man explained. ''Then the women take off their tracksuits and jerseys and spread their legs. They switch off all the lights, and in the dark they fuck and fuck so you can't sleep. No wonder the place is damp!''

''Sure, but as I told you, you've got to talk to the cooperative, it's their baby. Nothing to do with us.''

''Why don't you get someone to wave a flag, you hick?'' asked the tall man in the overalls. ''Or a trumpeter, you Slovak bandmaster! I've just had it painted red! But that doesn't interest him, no sir!'' he screamed in sudden amazement. ''He goes and practically kills a man and all *he*'s interested in is his wretched watercan!'' He strode up to the water cart and tried to inflict still more damage on the bent spraying attachment.

The driver in the corduroys looked on in dismay. ''What're you getting so uppity about?'' he asked, deciding to go over to the attack. ''I had priority, since I came from the right.''

The tall man let go of the metal pipe and gave a derisive snort. ''Don't make me laugh,'' he said, playing to the gallery. ''This clown comes arse-first up to the crossroads and now he talks about priorities!''

''Let me tell you something,'' said the old man with the officious mouth. He pulled a bottle out of his string bag and held it out in the direction of the first apartment block. ''Just let me tell you. I too have water in my cellar—this much water,'' he made a vague gesture, ''but do I complain? No, I just go and open a window. What's the use, anyway, water is an element, you can't argue with the elements.''

''That's all very well, but they don't just fuck in silence, they make a terrible racket and the women giggle and shout such obscenities that you can't go to sleep until the morning. I don't see why you can't discuss this,'' insisted the bald man. ''This is a medical matter. And there's my back, too—you know I have a medical certificate for it.''

''And anyway,'' the water cart driver thought he had hit upon the clinching argument, ''what were you doing here at this hour of the morning? Can't you see this is a dead end?''

''What a joker!'' shouted the tall man in the overalls sarcastically. ''Are you asking *me*, whom every child in this neighbourhood knows?'' He was trying to hold the twisted remains of his mudguard in front of the other driver's eyes. ''See that paint?'' he demanded. ''That's the best Dutch paint there is. And I'll expect you to pay for the lot.''

Recognition dawned. This, I realised, was Mr Holý himself!

''What do I care?'' shouted the man with the string bag. ''Your back, indeed! Why not your knees? You know, I told them right at the beginning that they'd have difficulties with you, and you'd be the only one to complain about the damp. Tell me, why doesn't the damp worry the others?''

This was really no place for me, as this was hardly the time to bother Mr Holý with my trifling problems. But I stayed, impelled by a sudden impulse to take a look at the fence behind which stood the scrap yard. Not that I saw anything, nor could I hear any sounds on account of the noise made by all these representatives of the male principle.

''So you refuse to do anything about it?'' asked the bald man.

''You bet!'' replied the man with the string bag. ''Let them fuck, if they enjoy it. So what if they make a noise? Doesn't seem to bother anyone else.'' He turned away from his companion and, looking grave, approached the water cart.

''If only it was *your* window,'' the other man shouted after him, ''you'd sing a different tune!''

The driver in the corduroys was standing there alone. ''You know where he's gone?'' he asked, his voice shaking with indignation. ''To fetch a policeman. A policeman! And we're supposed to be human beings—a dog wouldn't treat another dog like that!''

The loudmouth with the string bag assumed an important air. ''Quite right,'' he said. ''They'll soon establish who is in the right according to law.''

''What the hell was he doing here so early in the morning,

I'd like to know,'' lamented the driver. ''Getting in the way and getting decent people into trouble.''

The man with the string bag made up his mind. Leaving the woebegone driver to his own devices, he strode manfully to the pile of tin cans, stood there for a while as if admiring the feminine roundness of their bodies, then he bent down and picked up a handful, which he quickly deposited in his bag. Then he left the scene in dignified silence.

My eyes followed him as far as the little bridge. Casting a timely glance at the scrap yard fence, I was able to register the unexpected, fluttering arc described by the white coat as it was thrown by its owner in reckless abandon. As it sailed back towards the ground it caught by a sleeve on the phallus of the metal pipe and stayed impaled there, to be joined immediately by a vividly purple sweater, while a pair of rust-coloured plus fours merely soared into the air only to disappear again behind the fence.

I left my vantage point and walked slowly towards the scrap yard. When I was close enough to the fence to hear the loud moans and groans, about whose origin I could not entertain the slightest doubt, I suddenly remembered the present I had been given by the old man. I took the folded piece of paper from my pocket and unfolded it. Printed in golden letters in the centre of the large sheet there was this message:

HAVE FAITH IN YOURSELF!
Private Doctor of Philosohpy
Augustin Hovorka

I folded the paper again and put it back in my pocket. Without waiting for the familiar faces to reappear, I set off down the road dominated by that notice with its inscription, which had intrigued me ever since I was a small boy:

TRESPASSERS WILL BE PROSECUTED!

FRIDAY MORNING

An Orderly's Tale

(with a story inserted in a hatbox)

It was raining outside, that authentic autumn rain which starts some time around midnight and carries on for thirty-six hours, nonstop. It was only half-past twelve but I had nothing more to do, not since before ten—and even then all I did was help the staff nurse count the sheets and pillowcases. Partly on paper and partly on the shelves and in the store. We were 170 pillowcases and 215 bed sheets short, though only 153 coverlets were missing.

"There, you see, Mr Klíma," lamented the staff nurse. "Stolen, every single one of them!"

I tried to comfort her by saying I was sure we would find the missing linen lying forgotten in some cupboard or other, but to no avail.

"You'd be surprised," she said, "what gets stolen around here. Not even the beds are safe. They'll drag the thing at night to the fence by the woods and simply throw it over to the other side. Or take the time we were putting down the new linoleum. We had to move the patients out of one ward and had them lying on the floor in the corridor and were praying that the workmen would manage to do the job in one day, and what happened? During the night all the cans of glue disappeared, the workmen took offence and didn't show up for five days. Biebl took that glue, who else, but although everyone *knows*, how can you prove it?''

''What're you going to do about the linen?'' I wanted to know.

''Write it off, what else?'' said the staff nurse. ''Mr Klíma, you've no idea what people filch these days: drugs and plaster, paper and soap, and cotton wool and galoshes, and the quantities of food they carry away.... They'll take the chair you're sitting on right from under you if you don't watch out. Six have vanished in our ward this last year. And don't think that test tubes are of no interest to a thief, either—a whole crateful disappeared from the lab. Not to speak of crockery. Shortly before you started working here,'' the staff nurse continued, ''this circular was sent round all the wards.'' Taking a yellow sheet of paper from the drawer of her desk she read out loud: ''Owing to the fact that, in contrast to the high standards maintained by the majority of our employees, pilfering of socialist property has recently reached dangerously large proportions in our institute, culminating in the theft of the double doors to the garage, the management must inform you that we are forced to take preventive measures and that henceforth all bags taken out of the hospital will be subject to spot searches by the porter. We believe that the majority of honest employees will welcome this measure.''

''And *did* they start searching people's bags?'' I asked. No one had searched mine so far.

''What do you think!'' She waved a contemptuous hand. ''Didn't I tell you? People chuck the stuff over the fence, and someone's already there waiting and carts it all off. The very next day after this circular was sent round, C Ward lost all its toilet doors. What do people need so many doors for, I'd like to know.''

''Do you report these thefts to the police?''

"Go on! They'd need two cops to watch every employee. Last month they were going to install new radiators in A Ward. Seventy were delivered, and do you know how many were left by the time the workmen actually started installing them?"

"Fifty?" I deliberately quoted a high figure, so as not to spoil her fun.

"Thirty-seven!" she announced triumphantly.

"But that's terrible!" I said, feigning surprise. "The patients in A Ward will freeze to death."

"Oh no, that's all taken care of," she explained. "Knowing that things get stolen, they always order at least twice as much of everything as they need."

"In that case," I calculated, "they should've had some radiators left over."

"You must be joking," she said wearily. "They of course had to order a hundred and fifty, but they didn't get half of that because the supplier knows they're ordering twice as many as they need, and radiators are in short supply. On the other hand, the thieves left most of the old ones behind—they were better than the new lot anyway. I shudder to think," she went on, returning to more immediate concerns, "what'll happen when I start counting the clothes tomorrow. Last year we were almost 300 nightgowns short. How else do you think that man Biebl could afford to build his new house?"

We had finished counting the linen by half-past nine. I then took one old gent to the X-ray Department, and had since been wandering around the building, trying to find a suitable place to hide where I could continue undisturbed my reading of Stalin's daughter's memoirs, which a friend had lent me for two days. I tried it first in the cellar but found unexpected activity there, as a delivery had just been made of bales of cotton wool and other medical supplies. I read for a bit, standing up, outside the carpenter's shop in the next pavilion. This was a most pleasant place, warm and quiet, and on top of that permeated with the smell of wood. But my conscience troubled me—what if I was needed on the ward? So I went back there every quarter of an hour to see, but running back and forth in the rain was no fun. I therefore found refuge in No. 50, a small bare room which, when it did not provide a temporary resting place for a deceased patient, was used by the nurses for a quiet smoke. Here it was that I had listened in some amazement to Sister Vera, whose face was the most angelic of all the nurses at this hospital, telling dirty jokes.

But now it was almost the end of the shift, and I decided to make for the orderlies' washroom, where we had our lockers and which we could use as a resting room when on night shift. During the day you weren't supposed to hang around there, except to go to the toilet. I arrived just in time to see one of my colleagues, Biebl, standing by his locker and unwinding a long white piece of material that he had wrapped round his bare chest. It took me a little while but then I realised that it was a bed sheet.

"I'm sorry," I said, embarrassed, "I had no idea...."

"That's OK, glad you've come," he said, turning his narrow, bird's face towards me. "I need to vamoose before one o'clock. If they call from Emergencies, would you mind stepping in for me?"

"Oh, all right," I said, none too willingly.

"They won't call, you know," he assured me. "Dr Hák said he'd chuck out anybody who wasn't at death's door. But just in case; ... " He folded the sheet meticulously; he must have had a lot of practice because it fitted beautifully inside his small briefcase. "I've got to be at the school by half-past one, got to keep an eye on that little harlot of mine," he explained. "It's really terrible—I guess I'll strangle that little brat one of these days."

It dawned on me that he was talking about his daughter, whose photograph he had shown me only the other day.

"Just imagine," he went on, sawing the air with his arms, "she's only fourteen but she's got herself a boyfriend and is playing hookey. When I tried to talk her out of it she had the gall to tell her mother and me that she hated us. And next day, when the teacher called her to the blackboard, you know what she did? She was combing her hair, and so she says: 'Wait a minute, I'm just doing my hair!' But that's all over and done with now—she used to have hair right down to her waist, but when I heard about that combing business, my wife's elder daughter, her sister, took a pair of scissors and cut her hair off. You should have heard her cry! The little bitch. That's about the only thing that *will* make her shed a tear. The other day I broke my new fishing-rod over her, what I paid three hundred for, and she didn't bat an eyelid. The older girl, now, though she isn't even mine, my wife had her with her first husband, as soon as she sees I'm annoyed she'll apologise and promise to behave. But this one—she's made of stone, she is, a block of wood. I don't suppose there's anything would upset *her*. It's not as if I hadn't tried to be nice to her, but she just turned her back on me.''

As he spoke, Mr Biebl pulled two large cakes of soap out of the pocket of his white coat, then a pair of brand new rubber gloves and a packet of sanitary napkins, stuffing all his acquisitions neatly into his briefcase.

''It's all that boy's fault, he's putting her up to it. She even dared to say to her mother and me that we're a pair of old fogeys and she hates the pair of us. Would you believe it? That's what she said. And our next-door neighbour's daughter, she's also had a lot to do with it. A colonel's daughter, she is, but she's gone to work in a night club. If only you saw how those two wenches get themselves up and paint their faces. At school they don't know what to do with her. They told me, Mr Biebl, they said, the entire staff is at its wits' end with your daughter. She wrote a rude message with a ballpoint on her teacher's deerskin jacket. Lucky the guy had some sense. Never mind, Mr Biebl, he told me, it was an old jacket anyway. But it still cost me three big ones, had to buy him a new jacket, didn't I? And it's all that wretched boy of hers! Do you know he's hiding from me? But I'm going to find him, make no mistake. One of these days I'll catch them *in fla-granti*, and then he'll go to jail and she'll end up in reform school. The rotten cow. How did I come to be blessed with such a daughter, I'd like to know. She has a wardrobe full of the things her sister passed on to her, but will she wear any of 'em? Not on your life—not good enough for her ladyship, are they? She just uses that wardrobe to sit in—sits there all afternoon sometimes, can't get her out. And if you tell her off, she just laughs in your face. What can you do—she's a hopeless case and she'll come to a bad end.''

On this pessimistic note Mr Biebl ended his long diatribe. From his coat pocket he took a handful of coins and several crumpled ten-crown notes, which he had cajoled out of the dying geriatrics on the ward, and transferred them to the pocket of his leather jacket. He looked in the mirror and ran a comb through his thinning, pale hair, raised a hand in greeting, and walked out of the room.

At long last I was able to ensconce myself in the armchair, but I had hardly found my page in the book when fat Mr Mixa came barging in, a roll of election posters in one hand, a hammer in the other. ''Damn it all,'' he exclaimed, throwing the posters on the floor, ''I'm going to take a nap. Got a thirty-two hour shift today. That cunt of a staff nurse asked me to hang them up,'' he continued, pointing to the posters, which depicted a child's smiling face against a background of factory chimneys and combine harvesters. The slogan read: ''Elect the Party's candidates, for Peace and a Better Tomorrow!''

''I stuck three of 'em on each floor, but we only *have* three floors,'' said Mr Mixa, crossing over to his locker. ''So I nailed one on each side of the door at Emergencies—and I *still* have nine of the bloody things left.''

He took a bottle of beer from his locker, used his teeth to remove the top, and poured the yellowy liquid into his throat from on high. ''Hell, what a day,'' he complained as he took his shoes off. ''If anyone calls me, you know where to send 'em. Let 'em all go and fuck themselves.''

With this, he lay down on the white camp bed which was only supposed to be used during the night shift, and I tiptoed out of the room so as not to disturb his well-earned rest.

It was only a quarter past one. Luckily for me, a wooden bench stood in front of the washroom. The corridor was empty. Through the half-open door dead opposite I could see inside the Intensive Care Unit. Sister Tanya was in there, changing the drip on a stand. An elderly man in an old-fashioned black suit was sitting at the bedside of the only patient; this was strictly against the rules, as no visitors were allowed in Intensive Care, but that had nothing to do with me.

At last I was able to open my book and continue reading what Svetlana Aliluyeva had to say about her bloodthirsty father.

Before I had managed to read a single page, Tanya emerged from the room opposite, a packet of cigarettes in her hand. Seeing the book, she asked: "You mind if I join you?"

She had a thick mane of black hair which she wore in a tall beehive, and dark eyes whose size was accentuated by the use of eye-liner. The Lord had likewise blessed her with an ample bosom, and her lips were so thick that they no longer seemed sensuous, perhaps because these kissable lips parted to reveal brownish, decayed teeth. Yet, despite her ugly teeth—or maybe thanks to them—there was something touchingly gentle and appealing about Sister Tanya.

"Of course I don't mind," I said. "At least I won't be bored."

"It *is* a boring sort of day," she agreed. She offered me a cigarette, and when I said I didn't smoke she put away the packet. "I've such a long way to go, I'll get properly wet before I'm home."

"Where do you live, Tanya?"

"Out in Kobylisy. Takes me fifteen minutes from the tram stop. And the mud I have to wade through." She explained: "A year ago they dug the street up, to install gas they said. One day they just went and left everything the way it was."

"No gas?"

"No gas. We were told that our houses would probably be demolished. So there you are. What is it you're reading?"

"It's about Stalin," I said. It did not look as if the name meant anything to her. Tanya was no older than twenty-six, if that; she hadn't even started school when the dictator died, and in our part of the world deceased rulers are rarely mentioned, unless to be reviled.

"I've noticed that you're always reading something." She leaned across me to look at the book. Her thick lips moved soundlessly as she tried to read the foreign text. "You understand English?"

"Well," I replied with some reluctance, "that's not so difficult."

"I learned a little French," she said. "My mother wanted me to, but I've forgotten it all. Are all the books you've been reading in English?"

"No, I read whatever I can get hold of," I explained. "Last time it was Kirkegaard. It was a handy pocket size," I added hastily, in case she should think I was showing off.

And it was true, I did choose my reading matter according to size, selecting those books which fitted the pocket of my white jacket. Whenever opportunity arose during my working day, I'd pull the book out and read. This helped, at least partly, to assuage the feelings of discontent brought on by my new employment.

"Where did you actually learn your English?" Tanya asked.

"At school. And so on, I don't really know," I said evasively.

"Is it true that you've been there?" Tanya would not be put off.

""Yes," I admitted.

"In London?"

"There too."

She sighed and rose. "I think I ought to send Mr Lhota

home now," she said, pointing to the old man still sitting motionless by the only occupied bed. "The head doctor has given him permission. I think he used to be his tailor. He's been sitting here like this for three days. But the old lady's going to die tonight anyway. Tomorrow morning at the latest. I'm on night duty tomorrow," she said, obviously pleased that she would not be here when it happened. "Do you think it'll stop raining by tomorrow?"

"I'll give you a lift home, Tanya," I suggested. "Would you like that?"

"You have a car here?"

"Yes. It was raining so hard this morning."

"Well, I don't know...it must be out of your way," she said.

"I have a friend who lives near you," I said uncertainly. "I've been meaning to visit him."

"All right, I'll try and hurry so you don't have to wait for me." She vanished into her cubbyhole and I was free to carry on reading about Svetlana's daddy, how he bumped off his former friends and comrades.

At ten minutes to two I got up and returned to the resting room, where fat Mr Mixa had now been sleeping a full hour. I sympathised with him. He had to sleep off his last night shift and prepare for the next. I tried to slip by him as quietly as I could to reach my locker, but Mr Mixa slept like a guard dog. He opened his piggy eyes, glanced at me, yawned, and declared: "Shit, I could do with a good fuck."

I was just pulling my sweater over my head, and this enabled me to leave his announcement unanswered.

"Are you off then?" he asked, yawning again.

"Yes."

"Is it still pissing?"

"Yes."

"I've got this tremendous need for a bit of skirt. I must've dreamed about cunts or something," he said, sitting up. "That owl is on duty in Intensive Care, isn't she?"

"You mean Tanya?"

"That's right. Tanya. She won't put out, that one. Heaven knows who she thinks she is. A calculating cunt, that's what."

Mr Mixa worked as an orderly on the ward. He weighed at least two hundred fifty pounds, was about six feet tall, his age I could never estimate, but he couldn't have been much under fifty. His wife was a lot younger, she could well have been his daughter. She came to see him at the hospital sometimes, a good-looking woman with attractive, if somewhat coarse features.

I think she worked as a shop assistant. Whenever I saw her she was giggling at something, no doubt under the impression that laughing made her look sexy. In bed, or so Mr Mixa maintained, she demanded it three times—first with him on top, then from the left and thirdly from the right. Mr Mixa related all this in order to show how virile he was despite his age and his bulk.

"Who's on afternoon shift?"

"I have no idea," I replied truthfully.

"I bet it's Jana. And that's no good either, she won't oblige. She does it with the head doctor."

"Really?"

"He's a regular stallion." Mr Mixa got up, went to his locker, brought out a bottle of beer, removed the metal cap with his teeth, spat it out on the floor, and drained the bottle, making a gurgling sound as he did so.

"I'll have to give my old woman a ring," he said. "Who knows what she's getting up to in my absence. Have you seen her?"

"Yes."

"She's all right," Mr Mixa boasted. "fantastic in bed and she brings home money. Trouble is, she's too keen on blokes. The other day she comes and says why don't we go out and play canasta. You know what that is?"

"Yes."

"Can't understand how such a shitty game can amuse any-body," wondered Mr Mixa. "They don't even play for money. Can you understand that?"

"No," I said, wiping my shoes with a towel.

"It's one of the girls from her shop, they play it at her house. A snobby lot, her brother is a lawyer. They tanked up on gin and kept on about getting a straight canasta. And sud-denly I look under the table and see this bugger holding my wife's knee. So that was the end of that and we were off home. At home I bent her over a chair and took my belt to her. For a fortnight," Mr Mixa reminisced with evident pleasure, "we only did it from the side. And she couldn't sleep on her back. At least she didn't snore." Recalling his marriage bed Mr Mixa yawned. "Nobody called for me?"

"No," I said.

"Well, why the hell don't you piss off," he urged me. "Be glad you're off duty. I have another sixteen hours to go. If there's a frost in the night and women start falling down in the street, heaven help us."

"I shouldn't think we'll have a frost," I said. "On the radio the forecast was for a warm front."

"Those bastards lie even about the weather," Mr Mixa dismissed my reassurances, then yawned once more. "This week I'll notch up ninety-six hours." And he stretched out again on the camp bed. "That's three thousand, not counting tips." He shut his eyes and I went out into the corridor to wait for Tanya, who was changing.

Never in my life had I thought I would one day be working as a hospital orderly. But one of my former journalist col-leagues warned me that the authorities intended to deprive most writers in my position of their insurance and have us indicted for "parasitism". And although I knew that this col-league had never been the most reliable source of information, being too fond of making things up, this did sound plausible and I decided to look for a job. A surgeon of my acquaintance pro-mised to ask at his hospital, and since he was a top man there and they needed orderlies, they invited me for an interview.

It all happened so fast that I felt trapped. My insurance remained untouched, I was in the middle of a novel, and if the truth were told, being an orderly did not appeal to me in the least. But the people at the hospital seemed so keen to take me on and provide me with a living that I could not bring myself to refuse. I took the job on a part-time basis so that it would not affect my insurance and went to introduce myself to the staff nurse in Surgery.

The staff nurse was a lady of about my age and of dignified appearance. She read my file and discovered that I had been to university, lectured at an American college, spoke four languages, and was a writer by profession. She gave a deep sigh. (Obviously she feared that too much education would only get in the way of an orderly in coping with his duties.) She asked if she was to use my surname or my Christian name when addressing me, and then she tried to fit me out with a uniform. All her efforts to find me a white shirt and jacket with all the buttons intact ended in failure. ''Why, there's two pairs missing again,'' she exclaimed. ''God Almighty, it's that Biebl again, I'll warrant.'' She produced a pair of newish trousers which even looked as if they might have been starched, and asked me kindly to sign for the garments I was being supplied with because ''we've got to keep some kind of order'', and I duly became a hospital orderly.

It was so easy—I don't think you could as easily turn into anything, except perhaps a corpse.

At last, Tanya appeared at the end of the passage, wearing a long fur coat and a fur hat. I hardly recognised her.

Outside it was still pouring. I switched on my lights and windscreen wipers, and we were off. Tanya took off her hat and sat there in silence.

''That lady at whose bedside the old man is sitting,'' I asked, ''what's wrong with her?''

''Cancer of the liver,'' she replied. ''He just sits there all the time, holding her hand. Doesn't eat, doesn't speak. Today

I at least made him drink a mug of coffee. He won't outlive her by more than a few weeks. You know, there are people who get so used to one another that they can't go on living on their own.''

She unbuttoned her coat, finding it very warm in the car. ''They tell me you also write books,'' she said without looking at me.

I wondered who could have told her—the staff nurse, most probably, she had seen it in my papers.

''I've never read anything of yours,'' she went on. ''I don't read a lot, but the girls said they'd read something.''

''That's quite possible, my books used to get published here.''

She was silent for a moment. ''I bet you know lots of famous people,'' she started on a new tack.

''Oh, I don't know. Not really.''

''We get all kinds of people here,'' she said. ''From the films and the theatre. Krejča, for instance. You know him, don't you?''

I said I did.

''But they usually stay only for a day on my ward,'' she said regretfully. ''And mostly they're unconscious. The girls upstairs were annoyed with him, didn't give them anything, they said, only sent tickets for the theatre. They say you've been to America.''

''For a while.''

''When?''

''I came back in seventy. In the spring.''

''Why did you come back?''

I find this question very tiresome. ''For a writer it isn't easy to live in exile,'' I said.

''But they won't let you write anyway, will they?''

''That's right.''

''I came back too,'' she said.

''When?''

''Just after it happened. You see, I had a friend. . . . '' She hesitated, then went on: ''He was my fiancé. And when they came in August, he just threw a few things in his car and we left. But I had my father here, and my fiancé couldn't find a job straightaway, and so we agreed that I should go back for a time. Then it was quite easy.''

''What did he do, your fiancé?''

''He was a doctor,'' she said. ''A gynaecologist. He was quite a bit older than me. At least your age.''

''Why didn't you rejoin him?''

''Well, at first he wrote to me,'' she explained, ''but then suddenly, nothing. I think he's over there, in America, now.''

By this time we had driven over Troja Bridge.

''It's the next one on the left,'' she said. ''and then up the hill. Anyway, I wouldn't want to live there.''

''Why is that?''

''I don't know, I guess I'd be scared.''

''Oh, you would get used to it.''

''And who knows, I mightn't find any work.''

''You like what you're doing?''

''Sometimes,'' she said. ''It can get very tiring. Like when I'm on morning shift and then on night duty.''

''Can they do that?''

''There's a shortage of nurses,'' she said. ''In a way, it's quite good. I don't go home and I save two hours travelling. But sometimes I feel it's all useless and that I can't go on. I expect you know the feeling.''

''Yes, I do.''

''My mother always used to say that love and kindness were the best healers.''

We must have reached our destination, for she pointed at a small, dark house. ''Here it is, thanks very much.''

I stopped the car. Taking off her glove, she held out her hand. ''That was very nice of you. Thanks. Or . . . would you like to come in for a coffee?''

''I don't drink coffee.''

"I suppose you're in a hurry. To see your friend, I mean."

"No, not at all."

Her room was tiny, but it was still as cold as a barn. She sat me down in one of the two armchairs, switched on the heater, and went off to make me a cup of tea.

The room was quite ordinary: a few flowers in a vase, a couple of cheap landscape prints in standard frames, and a handful of books on the shelf that had been produced by our controlled publishing houses. Everything was spotlessly clean, like a hospital ward before the doctor's rounds. But the furniture was modern and surprisingly tasteful. A wooden cross above the door.

"My father had those wardrobes made for me," she told me. "Very expensive they were, too. Would you like to listen to some music?"

I left it to her, and she brought a record by Penderecki.

"My father's wife is working this afternoon, so we can play it," she said, putting on the record. "She can't stand me, can't stand anything I do."

"Your mother died?"

"Almost ten years ago. She had been ill a long time, then a whole year in the hospital. She used to write me lots of letters when she was in the hospital. Lovely letters. She was ..." Tanya's eyes filled with tears and her lips trembled. She got up quickly and went out to fetch the tea.

I listened to the music. When I was a boy—or rather a teenager—I used to have fantasies about making love to a nurse in a hospital. I would be lying there as a patient. I didn't imagine any particular illness, but whatever it was, it was no obstacle to my amorous pursuits. The nurse had her little room on the ward, and in that room she had cupboards full of medicines and, heaven knows why, a screen. At night she would come for me, gesticulate for me to follow her, and I would accompany her to her room. There, she allowed me to take off her white uniform. Then I carried her behind the screen, where there was a white doctor's couch. The rest does not require description. I have no idea why I should have chosen an anonymous nurse for my dalliance, probably because in my mind she combined maternal and virginal virtues, as befitted her mission of mercy. But all that was twenty years ago and Tanya had left her uniform at the hospital. Not to mention that there was no screen in her room.

She brought in the tea and delicate porcelain cups with Chinese ornaments. She had changed into a thin, crocheted blouse in which she must have been desperately cold.

"Doesn't the work you do at the hospital bore you?" she asked me.

"I haven't been there all that long."

"I see you sometimes in the morning when you're taking out the rubbish. I wouldn't think you'll last a long time."

That was a prediction I could not, in all conscience, argue with. My contract expired at the end of the year, and I certainly had no intention of renewing it.

"Orderlies never last long," she said. "Mr Mixa, he's the only one because he works on the ward and gets a lot of tips. Otherwise we get nothing but jail-birds. Take that Mr Biebl! Five times he was manager of a restaurant and every time he got chucked out because his books didn't balance, and in the end they locked him up. Came to us when he got out. He's a terrible thief and dreadfully rude to people, but they can't find anyone better."

"Well, it's hardly surprising," I said. "Who'd want to work for that kind of money?"

"They say that you're very nice to people."

"Who're they?"

"Oh, I just heard it. But then, you're not really an orderly, are you?"

It was true that I tried to treat the people who had been briefly entrusted into my care as kindly as I could, to show at least a little interest in their problems. But as often as not my main concern was to snatch a little time for my reading. It certainly was not in my list of duties: be kind to the patients.

They didn't ask that of me, nor could they for the wage they were paying me.

On one occasion I had to push an old lady on her trolley from one department to another, and finally move her and her possessions to another ward. She was all yellow from her liver ailment, and we all knew she had only a few days left. She pleaded with me to take her hand. Please, I'm all alone in the world. The idea did not appeal to me, she was so repugnantly yellow and stank of urine, but I took her hand and stroked her yellow forehead while we waited for yet another futile examination. She lay there with her eyes closed, silently squeezing my hand.

When at last they accepted her at Internal Diseases (for some reason every department does its damndest to get rid of those who are about to die—maybe they keep some kind of statistics, and those with the fewest mortalities are in line for a bonus or at least a recreation voucher), she wanted to give me a ten-crown note. I refused to take it (Tanya was right, I really wasn't an orderly), but she begged me to take it and to come and visit her.

I promised to come and did not take the money. And of course I never came, I had too many other unsavoury jobs to do, too many tasks which seemed humiliating to me. Maybe had I accepted that ten-crown note I would have visited her, while others would have taken the money and still not come. They had been leading this humiliating existence for far too long, and for them there was no escape. And so they came to see it as a rule of life, their relations with others being governed by it.

The record had stopped playing a few minutes ago, I ought to get up and leave.

"My mother," said Tanya out of the blue, "wanted them to call a priest, but they didn't."

"Why didn't they? Is that not allowed?"

"They just didn't," she said. "According to them, there is no God, so why call a priest? I wasn't allowed to stay, either."

"How old were you then?"

"Sixteen," she said.

"I suppose they didn't want you to see her die."

"That's not the point, is it." She used a handkerchief to dab her eyes. "Why don't you tell me about America?"

"Tell you what?" I asked, surprised.

"Anything you like." She was looking at me with kindly, devoted eyes. Suddenly I realised that this was a very lonely and unhappy girl.

"What do you do when you come home from work, Tanya?"

"First, I look if I've had a letter," she replied promptly, as if she had been expecting the question. "Then I run the vacuum and have a shower. When I've had something to eat, if she isn't in, I'll put on a record. Sometimes I have a chat with my father, if his wife is working in the afternoon. Or we might go to a film together. But we don't do that often nowadays. His eyes hurt him."

"What about television?"

"No, I don't like watching that, it annoys me. It's all a pack of lies. All the time they show you how beautiful life is, and people aren't at all nasty—everything is so artificial, so false. Sometimes I read over old letters," she added, perking up noticeably.

"Do people seem nasty to you?"

"I wouldn't want to judge anybody," she replied.

We were silent for a while and could hear the rain drumming outside.

"Men are crude and the women do their best to keep up with them. And there are things that no man would do, only women."

I must have looked sceptical, because she added: "If only I could tell you, you'd be surprised."

"What do you mean?"

"Oh, but I can't!" She poured me some more tea and

flashed me a smile so that I should not think she had been curt with me.

"Why can't you tell me?"

"I hardly know you," she said. "What if you go and print it somewhere?"

"How could I, Tanya?" I reminded her. "I'm not allowed to print so much as a line. Not for five years now."

"All right, so you'll say something at a meeting."

"I don't go to meetings."

"Aren't you afraid that you'll get into trouble?"

"No, I'm not. I am in far worse trouble, anyway, and there's nothing I can do about it."

"All right, I'll tell you," decided Tanya. "But some other time. Anyway, you haven't told me about America yet. I love hearing about foreign parts."

And so we drank tea and I told her how I had taught in Michigan and visited a Tao commune, and about an eccentric play about Che Guevara and about my own American first night. It had been a long time since I had last had an opportunity to talk about these things, and suddenly I found myself remembering long-forgotten details. Now, at this distance, to a man whose plays had been performed over there and who was now reduced to removing soiled sheets every morning and collecting other people's urine and other people's cancerous tissue, that distant land appeared quite unreal.

"What a pity I didn't know you then, when you were there," said Tanya when I had finished. "You could have sent me a postcard or a letter. I bet you write beautiful letters."

"I write very few letters," I said. "I hate writing letters."

"Oh, I *love* letters." Tanya got up and opened a wardrobe, from which she took a large hatbox. "This is where I've kept all my letters ever since I was a little girl." She fished in the box and, at random, pulled out a letter and started to read:

"Fairy tale,

I expect you will be surprised that I'm writing to you so

soon after we parted. But I just had to write and tell you how marvellous it was when we returned from our expedition to your castle and some mysterious power placed that magic root in our path. How splendidly we lost our way!''

She put the letter aside and said: ''I was thirteen, my best friend and I exchanged letters like that. Here I've got post-cards signed by famous people. And some of *his* letters. He only sent me six.''

She picked up a batch of letters tied with a gold ribbon, but replaced them without untying it. ''That's the last I heard of him. But I had lots of letters from my mother. I read them to myself whenever I feel depressed. She always ended her letters with a fine sentence, like: Take good care of your soul, Tanya. Or, Be nice to people and the Lord will repay you.''

It had grown dark, with only a little light penetrating the glass door from the hall.

All I had to do was to reach out and embrace her. I was sure she would not resist. Maybe she was expecting it, wishing it even. She was one of those women who, consciously or more likely instinctively, build a barrier of nostalgia around themselves. And more than an embrace she probably desired love. I got up and said: ''I'll write to you, Tanya. At the earliest opportunity.''

''A postcard will do,'' she said.

''I'll write. I promise.''

I started writing the letter that very evening. I finished it by next Tuesday when I was again on duty. I typed it out and put it in an envelope. It went like this:

Friday Morning

No one took any notice of the old man, not until they took the old lady, her skin all yellow, her cheeks and eyes sunken, all trace of life dimmed by pain and morphine, to the Intensive Care unit, where hopeless cases were sent to die. He had gained permission from the head doctor and in the morning arrived in this gloomy place, full of moans and stench. He pulled a chair to the sick woman's bedside, sat down, and stayed there, hardly moving for hours.

"You don't have to sit here all this time, you know, Mr Lhota," said the nurse the first day. "Your wife doesn't know you're here anyway."

"Perhaps she'll wake up?" he said.

"Why don't you sit in the corridor," suggested the nurse. "At least you'll have company. And we'll call you as soon as she comes to."

But he stayed. He sat there, gazing intently at the yellow, creased face of his wife, occasionally rising to wipe the perspiration from her face. Then he brought his chair even closer, took her limp, unfeeling hand, and remained like that until the evening. At first they found him irritating, like an alien object in a familiar space, but then they grew used to him as one does to alien bodies. It did not even occur to them that he might be feeling hungry or thirsty. He was, after all, a healthy man, and they had enough to do with the sick.

And he sat there looking at his wife's countenance, which was undergoing a rapid transformation, becoming less and less like the face he knew. And even though he knew that nothing could now halt the change, nothing could slow down that withdrawal and fall, it seemed incredible to him that it was going to happen, that it was going to happen in the next day or two. Only now did he fully realise what a boon it had been to be close to that familiar face, and he felt a deep sadness that during all their years together, during all of forty years, he had found so little time to gaze at it as he was doing now. And yet that face had accompanied him throughout his adult life. It now seemed to him as if he had spent almost all his time away from it, away from her eyes and her voice. What did she do all those long evenings while he sat at meetings at which various speakers promised happiness and a decent, dignified, even prosperous future; all those afternoons he had spent at the Sparta football ground; the Sundays and holidays he had given to the brass band, marching with it and thumping the big drum? Astonished, he found that there were whole periods of their life together when he could not remember his wife, did not know what she did, could not recall her face, or a single event, good or bad.

Yet other moments were lodged in his memory so vividly that he could recall every detail, with colours, smells, sounds, and the sensation of warmth, so that in the midst of the stench on the ward he was conscious of the sweet scent that flooded the room at the inn where they had first slept together—before their wedding—coming from the garden in full bloom and investing the night with a warm glow that enveloped their bed and breathed on their naked bodies.

"Mr Lhota," the nurse said to him, "it's almost eight. You must go home now, get some sleep."

"I beg your pardon?" he asked.

"It's evening," said the nurse. "You can't stay here."

"But what if . . . if during the night . . . ?"

The nurse looked at the yellow face on the pillow and said: "No, not yet. Have no fear."

And so he went home, to make himself some coffee on the gas stove and cut a piece of bread from the loaf he had been using all that week. It was frosty in the apartment and not worth his while to make up a fire, so he climbed into bed and surprisingly quickly fell asleep, as if he had done a hard day's work.

Next morning he woke up—as he had done for several decades—shortly after five, and as soon as he had had a little breakfast returned to the hospital. He sat down on the chair which no one had moved away from the bed, and took the sick woman's hand. The life of the hospital went on around him. The nurse made the rounds with a syringe in her hand and, like some monstrous mosquito, deprived the unconscious bodies of still more blood (only to replace it later by the bottled blood of others), a doctor came to read the notes and prescribe drugs, and he was immediately followed by the dietitian with a tray full of plates, but she went away again because there was no one left here who was still able to eat. Apart from Mr Lhota, of course, but no one took any notice of him. At last his wife opened her eyes and gave a loud sigh.

"How do you feel?" he asked quickly.

Her lips moved but no sound came from them, and her eyes closed again.

The air in the room was almost unbreatheable and he felt queasy. But he did not budge, accepting it as a necessary evil, a sad but unavoidable fact like death, or perhaps like a hospital. When he was eighteen he was sent to fight in the war, and he was wounded by a shell fragment the very next day after he arrived at the front. They took him to a field hospital near Pest, his first and also his last experience of a hospital. It did not occur to him that it was half a century ago, that nowadays there was air conditioning in the homes of the wealthy and in many a useless meeting hall. But he recalled how, very many years ago, they had been invited to the wedding of a cousin of his wife's down in the Bohemian Forest, and how when they got off the train she had said to him: "Just feel that air!" or words to that effect. It was evening and the sky was clear and full of stars, and it seemed as if all that sweet-scented air came down to them from somewhere in outer space.

The dietitian with her tray appeared in the doorway and vanished again. The yellow face on the pillow did not move. Not a flicker of consciousness.

He had not always been faithful to her. It happened several times, and when it did, he at least felt that something serious had taken place. He felt pangs of guilt and at the same time an illogical anger against the woman he was deceiving. Once he actually considered leaving her for the other woman, but he did not and later it all seemed much less significant, the other women gradually faded from his memory, he forgot those long-ago treacheries, the tricks and the lies. Now they all came back to him in a rush, and they appeared base but also ridiculous, and it was as if now, face to face with his dying wife, he was again committing all the old sins, again losing himself in a welter of lies. The terrible thing was, he could not communicate this, could not confess, and the lie thus became irrevocable and unchangeable.

The sick woman moaned. Leaning over the bed he whispered: ''Can I get you anything?''

The nurse dragged the stand over to the bedside and attached a bottle with the saline drip. She stuck the needle in the patient's arm, and he watched as the clear liquid slowly flowed through the transparent tube.

He thought that, in comparison with those few days or perhaps months when he had betrayed her, the time he was faithful to her was incomparably longer. But, he realised, you cannot weigh infidelity against faithfulness this way. Infidelity was an act, while faithfulness merely a state. Only another act could probably cancel out infidelity—but what kind of act? An act of love, most likely.

He tried to recall something good and kind, if possible some loving act of his. He remembered how he had made her a coat even though he was no tailor, but could that really qualify as an act of love? He had sewn that coat because it was cheaper than buying her one.

They had gone out dancing together and he then saw her home at night, even though he was sometimes very tired and had to get up at half past five, but that was no unselfish act on his part, for their way led through a park and they were able to kiss leaning against a tree or even hide in the bushes for a hasty bit of lovemaking. It seemed strange to him now that once they were young and strong and her hair was long and thick and her skin soft and white, arousing his desire whenever he touched her.

On those rare occasions when she was ill he would of course cook her simple meals and even do the washing, but then she did as much for him all her life, even though she had a job of her own and would sometimes not come home from the factory until the evening. He had never stopped to think of that, being interested only in what he did with *his* time, not she with hers. Now it occurred to him that her time was never filled with joy. But he did not accuse anyone because of this—not even himself. He could not imagine life taking a different, or a happier, course.

Another evening came, and he rose and, his gait somewhat unsteady, went out into the corridor, down two flights of stairs and out into the fresh air. The cool breeze almost took his breath away. At home he discovered that he had no more bread left, and so he searched in the cupboard for an old roll to go with his coffee. It was so old that even the bits of green mould with which it was speckled had dried. Tired and weak as he felt, he did not want to go to bed. So he left the table and went to the bedroom, where in a huge wardrobe he had several rolls of fine, expensive cloth. They would have to dress his wife, he realised, and she had nothing suitable for the purpose, in fact she had no clothes at all she could wear because she had lost so much weight that all her dresses were much too large.

He set to work cutting up the cloth, glad that he had something to do and could leave the lamp on and not have to go to bed.

Next day the old woman's face was even more shrunken than before, the skin had turned completely yellow, and her eyes had sunk deep into her face while her nose seemed more prominent and pointed. Her tiny hand bulged with blue veins, into one of which the nurse had connected the drip.

Pulling his chair closer to the bed, he arranged the pillow under his wife's head and straightened out the blanket. Gripped by a sudden fear that she was perhaps no longer alive, he bent over her to try and detect her breathing.

Her face remained quite immobile, and he thought that even though she was still breathing, perhaps she was no longer present in this room. Where would she be then? Most probably somewhere on her own—she must be used to that, she had really been on her own all her life, very much on her own. A woman who has no children remains alone, though that was something he had not given much thought to earlier, and if he ever reflected on her childlessness, then it was more of a reproach that she had deprived him of an experience available to most men. Now it occurred to him that she too must have suffered on that account, and that he had done nothing to relieve her suffering, on the contrary he had left her on her own on so many evenings. He recalled how on various occasions she had suggested that they go to the pictures, but he would turn her down, saying he wasn't interested in the rubbish they showed these days.

"Mr Lhota," the nurse was speaking to him, "why don't you go for a walk? She doesn't know you're here, so why don't you?"

But he stayed. When the dietitian looked in at noon with her tray full of plates, he grew conscious of hunger but ignored the pangs. Also, it was hot in here—made him feel unwell. They should open a window for a while, but the window was huge and too much cold air would flow in. So he at least leaned his head back and closed his eyes to give himself a rest, and at once he was transported to another time. He saw the room in which he had spent his childhood, but he saw it at the moment when his mother was about to die. That was a very long time ago, more than fifty years had gone by since. Two great wars, people had started to fly and drive in cars and build high-rise buildings and use electric light, and yet at this moment he thought he could smell candles and garlic, eiderdowns and the herbs which his mother dried behind the roof beam by the door, and outside there was a complete, unbroken darkness. From that darkness emerged individual figures, people he had not thought about for years: long dead relatives, his two sisters as little girls, and a woman neighbour whose name he could not recall, and finally the priest in his black cassock and hat, carrying a cross in his hand. At this moment the picture froze amidst the absolute silence of that occasion years ago. He could feel, across the barrier of expired time, the special solemnity of that moment, which he probably had not grasped then, being a socialist who knew that all priests were charlatans offering people nothing but opium, who knew that the only life we had was here on earth, the only kingdom vouchsafed human beings which need only be made over to them, and he was ready and willing to do so.

Nevertheless, he recalled, he did go to church, to accompany his mother on her last journey, their ancient church whose splendid dome soared high above the rooftops and above the trees and could be seen from any point in the neighbourhood. It was the last time, the very last time he entered a church, took his hat off and knelt; he was never to do so again because it conflicted with his convictions. God, after all, he had heard many times and he firmly believed, God had only been invented by men to keep others in subjection and humility.

Now he saw again that magnificent old church with its smell of incense, its wooden pews and the suntanned necks of the villagers ludicrously imprisoned in white starched collars; the organ thundered and women wept, and then the church bell pealed, scattering its sound far and wide across the countryside. The solemnity of the occasion was enough to make you cry, and indeed the tears came to his eyes, but he was crying because he had been so terribly young, his legs light and healthy, his eyes able to see into the distance.

"Mr Lhota," said the nurse. "I've brought you a little coffee."

It was the first time in a long while that anyone had taken notice of him as a living being. He took the mug and drank and then, though he tried to prevent it, he could not help sobbing out loud.

"You can leave earlier tonight," said the nurse. "But come tomorrow for sure."

He understood what she meant. He left as soon as it got dark.

He felt a strange anxiety as he waited for the bus. Not for himself, but for her. Now it was waiting for her—that horrifying, inexplicable condition when you ceased to be, when you severed all connection with the world of sound and smell and colour.

Suddenly he was not sure that he had not made a terrible mistake by keeping himself and her away from God all their life. One made so many mistakes in one's lifetime, what if he had made one in the most important question of all—that of life and death?

On Friday morning he arrived at the hospital before dawn. Nothing had changed in the room, she was still lying on the bed by the window, immobile and distant, unable to take in anything of what he saw and heard.

On the little table by his wife's bedside he laid the parcel containing the dress he had finished sewing in the night, then he sat down on the chair and again thought about God. He had never acquired enough learning—even though he had read a great deal when he was young—to be able to make up his own mind about anything as complex as he took God to be. He had had to rely on what others told him, more educated than he and whom he trusted. But now it seemed to him that most of those people he had trusted had cheated him. They had held out the hope of justice and a dignified life and even prosperity, but none of this had been fulfilled, and some of those people had later been exposed as traitors and criminals. He had long since lost all interest in them—the people and their fine speeches, their promises and their deceptions, he just did not think about them. Strangely enough, though, he had never asked himself whether, if they had lied to him about so many other things, they had not lied to him about God and the origin of the world. Perhaps nothing of what he had so firmly believed was actually true. Maybe even the earth did not go round the sun, and the stars were not so unimaginably distant, and the world wasn't billions of years old. In that case he had been wrong all his life about everything, and he had also led her into the same errors. Suddenly he had the odd feeling that it was because of him that she was now lying in this merciless room in which all the dignity of a human life vanished slowly on the conveyor belt of death, where no herbs gave off their scent and no prayer was heard, nor any words of encouragement or consolation, where no one said goodbye and no one cried, where all hope had evaporated except that which, from the bottles on the stand, dripped a day or two more into the veins of an unconscious and senseless existence.

The dietitian appeared in the doorway and left again, the rain drummed on the windowpane. He felt a weariness so great that it was as if he too were about to expire, as if he would never leave this chair.

It had never occurred to him that he needed to talk to her except about the most mundane things: about money, people they both knew, at most he would sometimes complain to her about his work, he really only talked because they were sitting together at the same table and it would have been a greater effort to keep quiet than to talk. Now, though, he wished he could speak to her, tell her about everything he had just been thinking, ask her forgiveness, and enquire whether she wanted a priest. Perhaps, he had heard that it happened that way in the very last hours of life, she would yet recover consciousness and he would be able to ask her. He must ask the doctor whether there was anything he could do to make this possible. Hopefully, he looked up at the drip, the big bottle from which the almost clear liquid was flowing into the old woman's veins.

The nurse appeared out of nowhere, bent over the bed, then she reached out for the drip and disconnected the tube. Only then did she turn to him to say: "No need to wait here any longer, Mr Lhota. The old lady has left us." That was all, with those words the nurse left the room.

He stood over the bed gazing at the face which had not changed in the slightest, it was just as still and just as yellow as it had been that morning when he arrived and when she was still alive. And of course it was quite different from the face he used to know. The transformation had been slow and scarcely perceptible, and like all such transformations was therefore not particularly harrowing. It did not even seem like a change, even though its end result was the difference between life and death.

It occurred to him that he ought to close the dead woman's eyes, as his father had done when his mother died, or to say a prayer, or at least say goodbye, move his lips, lament—but he was only a guest here, and so he only picked up the parcel from the bedside table and took a few steps back because some nurses had come in, bringing large, battered wheels which they leaned against the wall. Then they took the blanket off the bed and divested the dead woman of her nightgown, so that he caught a brief glimpse of his wife's emaciated body full of blue bruises where the needles had been lodged. And then they closed her eyes, covered her with a sheet, attached the wheels to the bed, and took her away.

He did not know what to do now, nobody took any notice of him. Perhaps he ought to go home, but on the other hand he felt there was something he should do here before he left, and so he followed the nurses to the room into which they had wheeled the bed with his deceased wife. It was a kind of store room, full of abandoned chairs, stands and wardrobes with missing doors, metal bed rails, and a large bale of cotton wool.

"Rudolf," a woman's voice called out beyond the door, "we've taken Lhotová to number fifty. She needs to be moved in a couple of hours."

"Oh Christ!" replied a male voice. "Why couldn't she hang on for another half hour? My shift is over and tomorrow's Saturday."

"OK, why don't you go home," came the woman's voice again. "We'll report that she snuffed it half an hour later."

He sat down on one of the chairs. The air was better here, spoilt only by the smell of cigarette smoke. This room was obviously used not only as a repository of useless junk and of deceased patients but also as a resting room where people could drop in for a quiet smoke.

He gazed at the bed which now, raised high on its wheels,

appeared monstrously tall. The sheet with which they had covered the body seemed to lie so flat that for a moment he doubted whether she was really still there.

There was complete silence all around him. He was aware at last—the realisation came to him gradually—that this was really the end, it was all over, he could simply get up and go. But he had nowhere to go and no reason for going. A saying came suddenly into his mind, a sentence his boss (when he was a young apprentice in those far-off days before the first great war) was fond of uttering whenever he picked up the heavy tailor's iron to put the finishing touches to a new gentleman's jacket: ''The end crowns our labours.''

He closed his eyes, and from depths he was not even aware of, from the very depths of his being he felt a desperate sorrow rising: like dogs, here we are, like dogs on a rubbish-heap. Who chased us out here, who is the master we served so faithfully, all those years we served—and now here we are on the rubbish-heap. He heard a soft rustling sound and, looking up, saw crows silently soaring against the grey autumn sky. Just like when they were lads and went racing out into the fields. the sight calmed him a little, and he waited for the familiar cawing sounds, but nothing came, nothing disturbed the silence all about him.

Then the door opened and a giant of a man came in, wearing a soiled white coat and dragging a curious metal trolley on rubber wheels behind him. He jumped, startled, from his chair and retreated so as not to be in the man's way. The man came up to the bed and pulled away the white sheet so that she again lay there naked, his dead wife, resembling a wax dummy. The man rammed his trolley up against the bed, opened the lid on top, then turned to him and said: ''My mate's away sick, would you mind giving me a hand?'' And so he stepped up to the bed and took the dead woman by the heels. She was so light, so very light, he could hardly believe it, although it may have been partly the other fellow lightening his load as he lifted the upper part of her body.

"It's been a hell of a day," said the man, wiping his ruddy forehead with the back of his hand. "Last night we had six dead 'uns. All women. Soon as autumn comes, these old girls fall like flies. One of 'em must have weighed half a ton, I didn't think I'd manage to load her." The man gave a huge yawn, then he slammed the lid shut on top of his trolley and wheeled it out of the room. Now he realised with a shock that she was being taken away from him, and he had not even said good-bye. He had done nothing, hadn't even dressed her in the new frock, hadn't given it to anybody for them to put it on her. It took him a while to recover, then he put the parcel under his arm and made his way to the staircase.

"Mr Lhota," the nurse called out, running after him, "we've looked for you everywhere. Your wife's things are here—will you take them?"

He stopped. "Now?"

"Just a minute," she requested as she left him. He stood by a large window and heard the doors of the service lift banging downstairs, then saw the trolley on its high rubber wheels down in the yard, being pushed by the giant in the soiled white coat.

"Here we are," he heard the nurse's voice behind him. She was carrying an armful of his wife's possessions, her dress and underwear, her dressing-gown and a pair of shoes with a little caked mud still adhering to them. He held out his arms and she added her load to the parcel with the new dress. "Now all we need is a signature," she said, handing him an official form. Noticing his astonished expression, she said: "But of course, we must keep some kind of order."

At a quarter to one on Tuesday afternoon I sat down on the bench outside our washroom. This time, apart from my own manuscript, I had with me Zweig's *Balzac*. The door to the Intensive Care Unit was shut, but I had ascertained from Mr Mixa that Tanya was on duty.

I had the long shift, until six in the evening, so I couldn't miss her, unless she was called away for some reason, which was unlikely at this hour. In any case, I could easily give her the letter some other time, yet I waited impatiently, almost like a lover waiting for his date.

About twenty minutes later she looked out of the door and, seeing me waiting there, smiled and disappeared again. Then she came out with her packet of cigarettes in her hand.

"Reading about that Stalin again?" she asked.

"No, about somebody altogether nicer this time," I replied. I felt a strange reluctance to hand over my envelope. "Did the old lady die?"

"Which old lady?" she asked. Then she understood. "Oh her, she died on Friday. I told you she wouldn't last."

"It no longer affects you?"

"You'd go crazy if you let it," she said. "I do feel sorry for them sometimes, though. When they're young. Or when I see somebody crying on their account."

For a moment we sat in silence, then at last I overcame my embarrassment and produced the envelope. "Here, I've written something for you," I told her.

She took the envelope and pulled out the sheets of paper. There were quite a few, a full dozen. "Is all this for me?" she asked, astonished, seeing that there was no name on the first page.

"Yes, for you."

"Can I read it? Right now?"

"If you like."

She spread out the twelve sheets and began to read.

She read slowly, and I tried in vain to deduce from her expression what she made of it. I would have done better to have gone away, but I could not pluck up the courage.

She was finished at last. She folded the sheets carefully, one by one, and laid them on the bench next to her. "You know," she said, as if carrying on an interrupted conversation, "I always try to do what I can until the last moment, even if I know there's nothing *to* be done."

"Don't the others do that?"

I was disappointed that she had not said a word about what I had written. Surely she must have some feelings about it. Remembering her critical view of our television, I had also hoped that she would appreciate my trying to write about life without embellishing anything.

She shook her head.

"How do you mean?"

"Oh, I don't know...." she said. "I guess you have a completely wrong idea about how things are. Everyone has. I used to have too. And my mother...poor thing...."

I was at a complete loss to know what she was talking about.

She was looking at me pleadingly. I noticed a tear on her left cheek, just below her eye. She wiped it away. "I didn't want to tell you last time. But I will. If you promise not to breathe a word to anyone."

I nodded.

"Upstairs, where you work," she said, "when they see that there's no hope any more, they mix up an injection, you know, barbiturates and things, they call it a cocktail, and when they give that to a patient, it's all over in a jiffy."

"Who mixes the cocktail?" I asked.

"That I'm not going to tell you, if you don't mind. But the doctors know nothing about it."

"Do *all* of them do it?"

She fixed me with her huge dark eyes. "But not a word to anyone!"

"Of course not. They'd all deny it, anyway."

She nodded. "Can I really keep this?" she asked as she got up, pointing to the papers on the bench.

"Yes, of course, I wrote it for you."

Tanya carefully replaced the papers in their envelope, making sure she did not crumple them before they went into her hatbox, while I counted how many days I'd be on duty before the end of the year when I would definitely leave, and while upstairs, the angelic Vera was mixing a deadly cocktail to keep in reserve for me, and while in the cellar below me crept Mr Biebl, on his way to steal the last remaining bale of cotton wool, and safely tucked away in our resting room, Mr Mixa slept to gain strength for his almost never-ending shift, and while all around me the world sped towards a better tomorrow.

"I'm truly grateful," said Tanya. "Thanks a lot."

SATURDAY MORNING

A Thief's Tale

The building site was situated at the bottom of a hill. Up there, the skeletons of high-rise apartment buildings in the process of construction towered against the sky like some monstrous ruins. We were supposed to be erecting only four prefabricated garages, but as yet not a single component had gone up. There was nothing to be seen except the damp emptiness of the four foundation ditches we had dug.

I was sifting sand together with Dr Králík, the foreman, or rather organiser, of our little working party.

Our other two fellow-workers, Drs Wolf and Merunka, were digging away a little distance from us. The sieve we were using for the sand was rusty, the mesh too dense. Or perhaps the sand was too wet and coarse. At any rate, most of it just kept falling back.

''There, we'll be finished in a jiffy,'' announced Dr Wolf, his smooth, pink face expressing contentment, as usual. ''Shouldn't the wood have arrived by now?''

The moment when I'd no longer be able to withhold the

bad news had come. Until now, I'd consoled myself with the thought that we would not get the digging done today, so that we'd have to leave the concrete until next week, by which time I would somehow manage to obtain the necessary wood.

"There'll be no wood today," I told them.

"Shit!" Dr Králík stabbed his shovel into the mound of sand. "Didn't you order it, then?"

"I ordered it all right."

"And did you slip those scoundrels a backhander?"

"Well, I only had fifty crowns, remember," I reminded my friends, the cautious doctors having decided that I was not to spend more on tips. "And I gave *that* to the blokes who brought us the cement day before yesterday." Procuring the cement I considered a particularly praiseworthy feat, although if the truth were told, it was not so much my doing as my former fellow student Libor's. All the credit I could claim was that I had an enterprising fellow student. "It shouldn't be difficult to find a few planks," I added. "Certainly easier than a load of cement."

"Well, I hope so," said Dr Králík sceptically. "When did they say we'd get the wood?"

"Next week."

"But *when* next week?" he wanted to know, displaying the annoying pedantry of his profession.

"On Wednesday," I lied, having accepted the vague assurance that we would get the material some time next week. As if I didn't know that next week they were also promising to deliver skis, typing paper, bananas, storage heaters, cocoa, spare parts for my car (and for other people's cars), typewriters, transistor batteries, tomatoes, boilers, floor coverings, accumulators, fisherman's capes, cotton undershirts, safety pins, vitamin C, wicker baskets, beefsteaks, flints for cigarette lighters, lawn mowers, distilled water and heaven knows what else.

Trouble is, I hate to have to bother about *things*. Whenever I pass a queue in the street, I feel dreadfully sorry for the people in it. Not so much because I know there is very little these days they can get without standing in line, but rather because they are so eager to possess material things, wasting so much time they could spend to better advantage.

Still, some people *like* to go around searching for things to buy. My former fellow student Libor, for instance. Way back in those austere post-war days when we were in school together he knew where to get pornographic pictures, printed exam answers with translations of Virgil's *Bucolics* and Cicero's tirades against Catiline, Swiss stopwatches, any number of American cigarettes, Swedish contraceptives, or Norwegian sweaters. And, for himself, a girl such as none of us others had even dreamed of. (I really admired him for this—I too wanted a girl, but no way could I get one.)

What he was able to procure in later years I don't know much about. At the end of our fourth year he flunked his Latin and physics exams and had to leave the school. This, of course, opened up new horizons for him, no doubt exceeding even his own expectations, never mind ours, those of us who had been more successful than Libor in mastering charades called *consecutio temporum*.

But who am I to talk, since I too had been unable to resist the temptations of our fetishist civilisation and had bought a motorcar. True, I have a love-hate relationship with the thing —I use it but I'm also afraid of it.

Shortly after I acquired the car I decided to take my family to the mountains. We drove in constant rain. After several kilometres we had a puncture, and this filled me with dire foreboding. I had to force myself to continue the journey, staring ahead fixedly in the expectation of the next catastrophe. Halfway to our destination I realised that the engine was making a strange humming sound. I was not entirely sure that anything was wrong, and so I asked the others whether they too could hear it. They said they couldn't be sure, either. I therefore stopped the car and went back (the car had a rear engine, that much I did know) to take a look. Opening the rain-washed bonnet, I saw various objects turning and clattering in there; the noise the thing was making now sounded even more sinister, and I could smell the hot odour of something burning.

I pulled out the oil gauge, the only move I had managed to master in my struggle with the monster. The oil came up way above the mark, but I knew there was no comfort to be found in that, since the engine was running. Then something else caught my attention: minute drops of something I was horrified to realise was melted metal came spouting out of the aperture from which I had withdrawn the gauge. I flung myself back inside the car, switched off the ignition, and announced dramatically: "The engine is melting!"

Now, of course I should have sold the car after this drastic experience; instead, I'm spinelessly trying to placate it by building it a garage.

It is unlikely that I would have thought of doing anything of the sort, had I not heard of three individuals who were preparing to build garages for their vehicles on a plot of land that would accommodate four.

I went to see Dr Králík, and the other two came as well. Dr Wolf was about my age. His first name was Vladimír, and he had the appearance of a good-natured somewhat rough-hewn countryman. Dr Merunka's name was also Vladimír, he was a little older, taciturn and self-contained, with so sickly a look about him that he must evoke either compassion or revulsion in healthy people, according to their nature.

I was shown into the sitting room. I had grown up in a technocratic household, and everything about this place reminded me of my childhood home. Everything in Dr Králík's apartment was neat, well-kept, and functional. Only the flowers in the window seemed slightly out of place, but those evidently belonged to the lady of the house. The lady of the house offered me coffee and cakes; Dr Králík, blueprints and budgets. He had it all worked out to the last millimetre and the last halfpenny. If I were to come in, they'd have to do all their measurements and sums again, but it appeared they were prepared to take the trouble. With four of us, he said, the cost per garage would be that much less. I couldn't tell whether they were ready to do all their calculations over again for the sake of those few hundred crowns or because they had read some of my articles when I was still able to publish and wanted to show their sympathy at my present plight.

Whatever the reason, they treated me in a most friendly fashion, even with respect. They referred to my editorial work, which I found rather quaint, since I haven't been allowed to do any for over ten years now.

And after that, every Saturday and Sunday, following a precise duty roster (worked out by Dr Wolf) I made my appearance at our building site on the weed-covered grassy plot at the foot of the hill.

The doctors ran among the tall weeds, with lengths of string, triangles, spirit level and measuring tape in their hands. All this effort just on my account. And to make matters worse, I was completely useless as far as any skilled labour was concerned. All I was good for was helping to hold the measuring tape, pulling up the weeds, or digging the earth.

Soon we needed to obtain our first building materials: cement and sand for the foundations, wires for the armature, iron beams, chipboard of all sizes and dimensions.

My three fellow builders worked in an institute just outside the city and returned home only in the evenings. Whereas I, who was—at least in their eyes—completely master of my own time, was their obvious choice as chief buyer, a thankless task if ever there was one.

Libor had first looked me up when I had completed my useless secondary schooling, as well as my equally useless philosophical studies. I was then employed in a publishing house, and many of my former and not so former acquaintances were in the habit of calling on me in order to offer me their literary efforts.

Libor came to see me at home, but as he was carrying a

bulging briefcase I was instantly suspicious of him. But I did him an injustice. The briefcase contained only a bottle of vodka, which he produced, saying he had just dropped in to ask how I was getting on.

In those days I was getting on quite well—and so, it seemed, was he. He was full of energy, had not yet put on excess weight, and he must just have come back from the mountains (people did not take holidays by the sea then) for he was beautifully tanned.

I thanked Libor for the vodka, still at a loss to understand why he had turned up like this, and as I was then a teetotaler, I poured only him a glass. He inspected the library the same way as he might have looked at some exotic items the purpose of which he found it difficult to understand, and then he sat down and started telling me how he had been making a living.

When he left the school he had gone to work as a bricklayer's mate, but got into some sort of scrape and retrained as a refrigerator repairman. This brought in quite a lot of money in tips, and also provided other fringe benefits (here he winked at me and paused in his narrative, giving my imagination time to picture an idyll set against the background of tiled kitchens where, in the space between the sink, stove and a half-demolished 'fridge, unsatisfied housewives eagerly discarded their dressing gowns and passionately threw their arms around him, sinking together onto the linoleum), and I could only nod understandingly when he added that in the end he found this way of life too tiring and so went to work for a coal merchant. While this was more lucrative, it was also more dangerous, as he had to entrust himself to possible stool pigeons and he therefore decided to find something less risky. He was now working as a car mechanic, and occasionally helped people to obtain cars without having to put their names on a waiting list. Should I perhaps be interested . . . he led me to the window and pointed down at the street, where outside the house I saw the expected sight in the shape of a large, shiny Mercedes.

At last I thought I knew why he had come to see me, and

this put my mind at rest. I was not interested in buying a car, and Libor, when he had finished the bottle, got up and left.

Thereafter, he would look me up every two years or so. As far as I could tell from his conversation and his appearance, he was doing better all the time. He grew quite obviously more prosperous, but he also seemed to age rapidly. His hair receded, and by the time he was forty he was practically grey. Only his eyes retained their youthful fire, betraying hidden passions. When I got married and applied for a cooperative apartment he already had several divorces and family villas behind him.

I was puzzled as to the reason behind his occasional visits. Perhaps he mistakenly thought I had some kind of influence, or perhaps I helped him to come to terms with some complex or other. Or maybe I just suited him as a good listener. I did not suppose that he was being sent to spy on me. Not only was there nothing to spy on, he never asked any probing questions.

Most recently he came to see me last week. Pulling a bottle of Scotch from his briefcase, he made himself comfortable in the armchair and asked me how I was doing.

I had lately been doing pretty badly, while he was now the chairman of a housing cooperative. Since I saw him last he had lost more hair and put on some weight.

I was building a prefabricated garage, whereas he was responsible for the construction of, among other things, eighty modern family houses. He had succeeded in obtaining a State grant for the project, so that a prospective house owner could build his dream home for next to nothing. But of course anyone wishing to join his cooperative had first to make it worthwhile to the management committee. I became apprehensive lest he start explaining some of the shadier transactions he was involved in, or enumerating the bribes he and his colleagues extracted from would-be house buyers. In keeping with the laws of conspiracy which I had learned to obey during my occasional meetings with my friends (as a rule in the middle of a forest or in a hired car, where we would discuss in whose apartment to stage a performance of *Macbeth*, or how we would copy each other's manuscripts, or even where we would have them bound), I warned Libor by means of an expressive gesture that it was more than possible that my apartment was bugged and he had better be careful what he said.

My fears seemed to amuse him. He said he felt absolutely safe here. For that matter, he felt absolutely safe in his own office. Even though, in order to avoid the prying eyes of his colleagues, he preferred to conduct certain negotiations elsewhere. For this purpose—and, as he said this, he leaned close to me, his alcoholic breath fanning my face—he had several "conspiratorial" apartments.

I wanted to know whether what he was doing was not very risky.

If only you knew, he told me, fixing me with his narrow, cunning eyes, *who* are the people I help to get houses. It was then that I understood that thanks to his powerful friends, *his* undertaking carried far less risk, no matter how much it might transgress the law, than my perfectly legal profession.

He then told me that he had recently remarried yet again (was it for the third time, or the fourth—I had lost track), his new wife was young and beautiful, and, what was more, she was the niece of a government minister. He actually named the minister in question, but I find it difficult to tell them apart, owing to their general lack of individuality and their easy interchangeability.

He switched there and then to talk of his new garden, which he had had built on several terraces, the middle one with a "music gazebo" containing the latest stereophonic equipment. However, he complained, he had as yet never had the chance of enjoying his music in peace and quiet—he was so busy working that he scarcely had time to live. And yet, he winked at me, there was no lack of opportunity. Thus I learned of a pretty barmaid, who had offered him thirty thousand crowns as well as her own person, and an even prettier dancer, who had confined herself to offering him herself—all this, of course, to gain the promise of an apartment in his cooperative housing project.

Intrigued, I wanted to know how beautiful women went about their business; what, I asked him, if they offered only their bodies?

So far, nix, he sighed. That dancer, he confided, if only you saw the legs she has! She sits down opposite you, crosses her legs, and fucks you with her eyes. You can't imagine how terrible it is to have to refuse her.

And, because I couldn't grasp why this refusal was necessary, he explained that if he were to start anything with the lady, he would be honour bound to get her the apartment she was after. And how was he to do that if she didn't hand him the requisite envelope? He himself would gladly forgo the bribe, naturally—but it had to be understood that he didn't decide these things on his own. Other palms had to be greased —and did I think he was going to cough up thirty thousand for a casual affair?

Well, maybe she'll bring something next time, I tried to console him; and then, acting on a sudden impulse (normally I have a low opinion of bribery and corruption), I told him that I'd been trying in vain for a whole month to get hold of some cement. A mere fifteen bags.

He just smiled and asked if he could use my phone. He dialed a number, uttered a few short sentences, and then told me where I was to go to pick up the cement.

"Christ, that's another five days down the drain!" cried Dr Králík, evaluating my success in obtaining the wood we needed. "and just when we've got such perfect weather!" he added, raising his eyes skyward.

Not that he was accusing me of anything, and yet I felt guilty. But I was ready with an emergency measure: "You know, when I was passing the building site up there," I pointed at the hillside with the monstrous skeletons of new tower blocks upon it, ''I couldn't help noticing that there are planks lying about all over the place.''

''You don't mean...?'' Dr Králík began doubtfully.

''They're no use to anybody,'' I assured them. ''Just lying there.''

''Are you saying you'd be willing to drag them down here?''

''Yes, provided someone gives me a hand.'' The idea of carting the dirty planks down that hill without assistance certainly did not appeal to me.

''But there won't be anyone there on a Saturday morning,'' interjected the usually taciturn Dr Merunka.

''Well, that's just the point, isn't it?'' I said.

''Oh, but surely we've got to pay somebody for the wood,'' objected Dr Merunka.

''Look, Vladimír, our writer friend is talking about *discarded* planks, right?'' pointed out Dr Králík. ''I suggest we go and take a look, and perhaps bring down a couple.''

''Oh, I don't know...if you all think it's the thing to do...,'' said Dr Merunka unhappily. He took his glasses off and wiped his forehead. ''I just don't want us to get into any trouble.''

And then the two of us were on our way up the hillside. Dr Merunka was silent, as usual, but he seemed more miserable than ever.

Silhouetted against the sky at the top of the hill were several small figures—children flying kites, which sailed colourfully across the grey sky, held by their invisible threads. Among them soared a strange, metallic-grey object consisting of a large middle globe surrounded by several smaller ones. It reminded me of a model of a none-too-complicated atom.

''Isn't that beautiful?'' exclaimed Dr Merunka. ''When I was a lad, I was always making kites, but something like this ...who'd have thought of it?''

He stopped to wipe his forehead again. His breathing was laboured and his sickly-looking face covered with perspiration.

''What a hill!'' he lamented. ''If you know Turzovka, that's another brute, just like this. Only it's five times as high.''

I was at a loss to understand the comparison. ''No, I don't know it, I've never been there.''

The house skeletons were slowly emerging at the top of the rise. The footpath fought its way through the thick undergrowth and tall grass, full of nettles.

''That's where Forester Labuda saw his vision,'' said Dr Merunka. ''Perhaps you've heard of it?''

''No, I don't think so,'' I said, taken by surprise. ''I'm sure I haven't.''

''Well, maybe you don't believe in that sort of thing, but I actually went there on my last summer vacation. I decided to visit the forester and find out for myself exactly what happened.''

''What was it he was supposed to see?'' I asked;

''Why, the Virgin Mary, of course. What else?''

''Do you mean to say that you believe in these things?''

''I'm a Catholic,'' Dr Merunka side-stepped the question, ''and the Church itself takes a very cautious stand on such matters these days.''

''There you are, then,'' I said. ''And did you find the forester?''

''I did. An extremely sensitive, well-educated man. He was very annoyed at all the fuss that people had made about the affair. They even wrote and duplicated a leaflet claiming that he had been instructed by the Holy Mother how to go about helping people give their children religious instruction. He was interrogated by the secret police as a result. And yet, he told me, all the Virgin Mary did was show herself to him—more like a picture. And a spring then appeared on that very spot.''

''And you really think,'' I asked, astounded by both the length and import of his revelation, ''that there's something in it?''

''Well, to tell you the truth, I did have certain doubts,''

confessed Dr Merunka. "But then.... You see, I suffer from an ailment I contracted while I was forced to work in the mines. But I won't trouble you with *that* story, I'm sure you have worries enough of your own. There were simply days when I couldn't catch my breath. And so I said to myself I'd go back there and try the waters of that spring. I went overnight, so as not to lose too much time. I have free rail travel, my wife is a railway employee. It was still dark when I got there, and I set off at once to the top of that hill. It was very cold, and foggy. It's in such weather that I have the greatest difficulty with my breathing, you know. When it's foggy, I practically suffocate, my face turns blue, and several times they had to take me to the hospital and give me oxygen. So I don't have to tell you I could hardly make it up that hill to the spring. I was choking by the time I got there, and dawn was just breaking. I stumbled and fell and just lay there. Then I leaned forward and drank the water. Just a few swallows, that was all, and suddenly the terrible weight was lifted off my chest and I was breathing quite normally, the way I hadn't done for years, not since I was a boy. I stripped on the spot—there was nobody about—so I took all my clothes off and sprayed myself all over with the water. I felt terribly cold in that damp morning air. And then I heard voices, and no sooner had I put my clothes on again, than some people turned up, two men and a woman, but they didn't seem to see me, they were looking upwards. So I looked up too, and I saw what they saw: two suns, next to each other, in the morning sky. I went down on my knees. The second sun disappeared, and the one that was left was like a rainbow—all colours, orange, purple, and then green. Can you imagine that, a green sun? Well, you don't have to take my word for it, there were four of us and we all saw the same thing!"

When Dr Merunka and I emerged from the undergrowth, the planks were lying directly in front of us. All white with dried concrete and lime. Apart from them, the place was littered with broken trestles and beams, with huge, rusty nails sticking out of them.

"You really think we can just take them?" asked Dr Merunka.

"Well, what else do you suggest? If we asked anyone's permission, they'd only laugh at us."

"Well, even so...," he protested. "I'm sure they can't cost very much."

"Of course not," I said. "But I'm sure they wouldn't be allowed to sell them, that's bound to infringe some regulation or other. At best we might find somebody who'd steal them himself and then *pretend* to be selling them to us. Anyway, today there isn't anyone here at all."

"Yes, that's all very well," said Dr Merunka, gazing in the direction of the children and their kites, "but it's against my principles to take anything that doesn't belong to me."

"Look," I tried to convince him, "I'll bet you anything you like that they lose far more valuable things than a few rotten old planks on this building site. These planks will only go to waste, anyway. At most, they'll throw them all on a heap and set fire to them, whereas we'll put them to good use."

"Well, if you really think so...," said my companion, his voice full of remorse.

I accordingly climbed up the pile of planks and started to pry loose the one on top.

The planks were practically leaning against the wall of the half-built house. When I reached the top I saw to my considerable surprise that one of the windows in the bare brick façade behind the planks was not only glassed in but had pink curtains in it. The curtains were only partly drawn, and I could see into the dark room with its bare, as yet unpainted walls. Behind a large table that took up almost half the room, five men dressed in their Sunday best were sitting on office chairs, all of them gazing raptly at the door.

Then, as one of them turned his face in my direction, I was astonished to recognise my one-time fellow student, Libor.

Just at that moment, the door opened and a girl in a

snow-white skirt and white top danced into the room. With one graceful leap she gained the tabletop, and made a deep bow in front of the five. Watching the professional movements of that lithe body I realised that chance had given me the opportunity of peeping inside one of my former fellow student's "conspiratorial" apartments.

My ear caught the faint sound of music, and the white apparition on the table began to pirouette wildly, her long, slim legs stamping on the wooden top, her narrow hips gyrating faster and faster. Then her gentle fingers undid the snow-white skirt, which dropped slowly down her thighs and calves until it came to rest on top of the table.

"Hullo there!" called out Dr Merunka from down below. "If you really think we should . . . then now's the time. The kids have gone, the wind was too strong for their kite."

"Yes, yes, in a minute!" I was staring at the dancer, still circling the big table. Under her white skirt she had yet another one, but this, I was staggered to see, was made of strips of green paper and bore a picture of what I took to be Prague Castle.

The five men were now stretching eager hands towards the dancer, and I imagined that at any moment they would fall upon her in order to divest her of the last remnants of her apparel.

"What's the matter up there?" I heard Dr Merunka's somewhat plaintive voice. "Can't you hurry up? Someone's bound to come sooner or later. . . ."

I caught my last glimpse of the dancer as she gracefully tore off several strips of paper from her remaining skirt and threw them into the faces of those happy five; then I bent over and threw down the first plank.

I threw down four in all, and then was interrupted in my labours by the stagey whisper of my companion down below: "Hey, come down quick, someone's coming!"

Before jumping down I cast one more glance towards that conspiratorial window, only to find that someone had pulled the pink curtains together. Through the tiny holes in the weave I fancied I could detect the mad kaleidoscope of green bits of paper and a confusion of naked bodies, yes, I even thought I could hear the muted cries of extreme, and in this case multiple, passion—and then I rejoined Dr Merunka down on the ground.

"Over there," he was saying, pointing in the opposite direction, and in the distance I saw an old lady accompanied by a small, limping dog.

"That's nothing to be afraid of," I said. "But let's go, if you wish. You don't have to carry anything, I'll manage on my own." And with these words I shouldered two filthy planks.

"Oh, come on, you can't," he said, and picked up the remaining two. As we made our way down the hill, my load hurt my shoulder, while grains of sand kept falling down my neck.

"It's not that I'm afraid, you understand," he explained from behind me. "I feel ashamed, that's all. I wouldn't like to adopt *their* way of life, you see."

After that, we proceeded in silence for some time. The silence weighed heavily on me, I felt that I had done him some injury, or perhaps caused him some terrible disappointment.

"Did you bring back any of that water?" I asked.

"You mean from Turzovka?"

"From that miraculous spring."

"Yes, I did. But it didn't do any good."

"I guess you've got to drink it on the spot."

"Maybe, or possibly it was a moment of special grace," he said.

Our colleagues welcomed us with open arms. We threw down our burdens, and while I told them about our expedition, Dr Merunka turned away and, as if feeling ashamed of himself, walked across to the other side of the building site. Sitting down on a pile of bricks, he wiped the palms of his hands and took out his sandwiches.

"These planks are just what we need," Dr Králík praised our booty. "But we need three times as many. Would it be troubling you too much if I asked you to go up there at least one more time?"

"Well, don't worry about me...," I replied, pointing cravenly at the lonely sandwich eater.

"You mean to say Vladimír wouldn't go again?"

"I shouldn't think so."

"Did he find it too exhausting?"

"No, more like against his principles."

"Oh, of course," said Dr Králík, the light of recognition in his eyes. "Vladimír has always been a funny fellow." He leaned across, close to me, and whispered in my ear: "Can you imagine, he actually started studying for the priesthood, but they locked him up just before he graduated—said he had distributed some Papal Bull or other. He got ten years, but then they released him when he'd done only six. Because of his asthma. And for good behaviour. He's a terribly decent and honest fellow. When he came out of jail he took an extra-mural course in engineering. Not that I have much faith in these extra-mural graduates, as a rule, but Vladimír is something else, he could give us all lessons.

"But still...." Dr Králík added. "Ten years for a Papal Bull. That's tough!"

SUNDAY MORNING

A Foolish Tale

I was awakened by the sound of a church bell, and immediately afterwards came the tap-tap of raindrops on the
window. This was a year rich in rainfall and police raids.

There were two churches in the village offering their servi-
ces. The one that was calling the faithful to prayer at this early
hour was Catholic, so its invitation did not concern me. Inso-
far as I had any right to call myself a Christian, I belonged to
the other lot. And it was the Protestant priest who had found
me this little room.

His name was Peter, and he was at least 15 years younger
and a head taller than I. He wore spectacles, size 12 shoes, a
heavy sweater which his wife had knitted for him, and used
the familiar form of address in conversation with me. I found
him rather too self-assured for a priest—he considered most
people foolish and poor in spirit (except two zany young men
who zealously attended all prayer meetings and whom he
treated with a truly pastoral tolerance). Otherwise, however,
he was a genuine human being and a kind father to his flock.

I got up and cautiously made my way to the low-set window.

The cottage belonged to the old widow of a glass worker. Every shelf and every little table was crammed with glass figurines, and every time I walked past them I was afraid I would knock one down and break it.

I looked out the window. The cottage was the last permanently inhabited building in the village. Further on towards the brook there were three more small houses, one completely dilapidated, the other two naturally taken over by visitors from Prague. They had repaired them after their own fashion, especially the one at the very end, whose walls were covered with spoked wheels, corn threshers and rakes and looked as if it were an advertisement for an ethnographical museum. I had no idea what it looked like inside, for its owner, a football coach by profession, was away touring Europe with his team. But it was not the cottage I was interested in at this moment, anyway. I was gazing in the direction of the brook, a wide, swirling torrent. Usually one would add: murky. It no doubt was, but at that distance and in the morning half-light I could not make out the colour of the water. It had already flooded part of the meadow between the brook and the football coach's cottage—all you could see now was the low bank of the narrow country road which led across a narrow wooden bridge to the other side of the brook and then disappeared behind the promontory of the forest.

It was raining hopelessly. I put my clothes on and went into the little kitchen to make myself some breakfast. The lady of the house had left to spend the weekend with her married daughter, leaving me completely on my own. I was thus able to write all day until the evening. But the more peace and quiet you have, the less work you do.

Not that I had enjoyed much peace and quiet this particular year. My friends had drafted a charter for the defence of human rights. Although I had not signed it myself—I felt that I had written enough texts of my own showing what I thought about the state of the world and about human rights—I couldn't escape responsibility for it. Our delightful mass media naturally began to denounce those who had signed the document and to slander them, while the ''working people'' immediately started to gather at protest meetings. I don't suppose they themselves knew what they were actually protesting against: whether against human rights as such or only those who had dared to invoke them. Most probably they told themselves what they have had to tell themselves for the best part of their lives: far better not to know and not to think!

In the next few days several of my friends had been arrested, others thrown out of work. In those circumstances it is quite a bitter pill to swallow that you, of all people, have been spared. But fortunately they soon went for me, too, in the major newspapers. They said that not only had I signed the Charter, but that I was an ideal go-between for the human rights movement because I was acquainted with all the leading personalities and could therefore inform the foreign press. And if a journalist failed to find me at home, he could always turn to my friend, an American film star, who happened to be in Prague. While this did not sound too logical, since I would have had first to acquaint my film star friend with all the leading personalities, it provided a good pretext for them to print my address in the papers. They got my address absolutely right. They also printed the name of the actress and of the hotel she was staying in. Whether they got *that* right, I don't know, for I had never heard of her before. Shortly after this, I started getting letters, two of them threatening, all the others enthusiastically on my side, and with only a few exceptions all of them anonymous.

A man who signed himself ''A Sufferer'' wrote: ''According to the election results, some 0.02% of the electorate did not vote for the official candidates—I calculate this to mean about 33,000 people. They were brave and you and your friends are braver still. Let them accuse you of having expensive, luxurious apartments, mistresses, and so on. If that is true, then you have all the more reason to behave selfishly and keep your mouths shut. You have not done this, and those of us who have suffered from the blacklisting feel very much in your debt. Don't let anyone tell you what to do— myself included. Even if everybody were to call you names or consider you to be acting like a lot of fools, everything you've written and published is true. Unfortunately, the truth is something this nation is too scared to utter, except in the privacy of people's bedrooms or over a glass of beer. And even then they want to be quite sure that the person listening to them is more drunk than they are, or that their wife won't divorce them the next day.''

One train driver concluded his letter with this request: ''I'd like to finish by asking you not to write the people of this country off just because there is no way we can help you publicly. How would anyone dare? Everyone's too frightened. You people know more about your rights, and also you are well-known personalities, who can't be dealt with as easily as ordinary citizens. . . . '' On the other hand, an angry man who gave his name as Franta Volek from Vyškov wanted to inform me that he had read about ''my criminal activities'' and that I had ''signed that bit of toilet paper. I've no idea who's behind these shitty plotters,'' he complained, ''and where all them criminals that belong behind bars or in a strait jacket think they get off wagging their slimy tongues at the expense of our beautiful country. Where were you, you chamber-pot, when we fought the fascists and risked our necks for freedom. Next month I'll be visiting Prague and I'll come and look you up for a little chat. I'll show you with me two hands how respected you and all those fuckin' friends of yours are, that's the only way to deal with your kind of arseholes.''

Of course, Franta Volek never showed up; instead I was visited more and more often by those who ''belonged behind bars or in a strait jacket''—I had never had so many visitors as in those days. We drank tea and discussed the latest events, that is, the latest house searches, arrests, interrogations, dismissals, and slanderous articles in the press to which we were unable—or I should say, not allowed—to reply. We also talked about the latest documents and news. From all over the world the news brought us encouraging statements by all and sundry, from the heads of state to our fellow writers. All this went a long way to help us forget our troubles.

My most frequent visitor was a professor—I don't know if I should mention his name, since I always referred to him only as Professor.

Until then I had known his name only from literature, having read his articles many years before in a philosophical magazine. Then, as they did with all who knew something and, more important still, all who were able to think for themselves, they stopped him publishing his articles and threw him out of the faculty. For two years he worked as a proofreader in a printing house, then he was sacked even from this job. He found work as a stoker, but a few days later a pipe burst and the boiler-room was flooded with water. The criminal police were called in and browbeat him to such an extent that he had a nervous breakdown. He was then fifty-six years old. During the war he had spent three years in a concentration camp (after the war a few years longer, but that did not count) and so he was entitled to an early pension. After two weeks in a mental institution he returned home, and as he also had asthma and diabetes, he was granted full invalidity for those few months before his retirement. He sat at home, translating Heidegger and writing polemical replies to the gibberish that passed for learned articles in our contemporary scientific journals. No one, of course, printed these polemics of his, so he typed them out in several copies and sent them to various authors and experts, their numbers being small enough for this primitive method of communication to serve its purpose.

Now, however, he had stopped composing his own texts, typing out various documents, articles, and reports about the injustices perpetrated by the authorities instead.

He usually came to see me in the morning, which was the time I had in less troubled days done most of my work. I could tell who it was when he was still outside my apartment on the stairs because I recognised his slow, somewhat heavy step. He would then give one long and two short rings on the bell, to show me that it was he and not someone I might be less happy to see. "I shan't keep you long," he would announce in the doorway. "I know you have a lot to do!" His lean figure appeared surprisingly rotund as he stood there.

When I assured him that, on the contrary, I wasn't doing anything, he took his coat off and began to pull various bits of carefully folded paper out of his pockets. "Now this is an open letter to the journalists, and this a letter addressed to all revolutionary socialists, have you seen them?" He was all out of breath, having climbed the steep hill and then the one flight of steps to my apartment.

I had not seen any of the documents he had brought, and he was pleased that he should be the first to show them to me. Then he took his jacket off and straightaway became much slimmer.

"How many copies do you carry at a time?" I asked.

"Well, I typed it all out twenty-five times, and you are my first port of call," he said. "Tell me, have you heard any encouraging news?"

I tried to recall all the encouraging news I could, of which there was as a rule far less than of the other kind; apart from which they usually bore only a passing relevance to our daily life.

"Doesn't all this typing take up a lot of your time?" I went back to his papers.

"Well, of course, it does take me a few hours."

"What a waste," I lamented, "for someone of your erudition and talent."

"Oh no, not at all," he interrupted me, "I enjoy it. In any case I'm incapable of doing anything else. I couldn't concentrate, you know. I read all that nonsense in the press and I can think of nothing else. And if I couldn't at least reply in this fashion I'd feel like a helpless slave. What's more, people are thirsty for the truth!"

"You shouldn't really be carrying all this stuff around in your pockets like this," I said. "What if you get caught?"

"Well, it isn't as if I was committing treason, is it?"

Next time I caught sight of him outside the house as I looked out of the window, his tiny figure trotting along down our deserted street. In one hand he held a magnificent black briefcase, all gleaming and new even at that distance.

"I've done as you suggested," he called out to me as soon as he entered, "and bought this for my papers."

"*All* of them?"

"All of them," was his proud reply.

"Five and twenty times?"

He nodded, handing the briefcase to me. "Just try and open it!"

Next to the lock there was a device with numbers on it.

"You can open it only if you know the combination?"

"That's right, the combination," he exclaimed joyfully. "And should they catch me, I'll simply say I've forgotten it!"

"Oh," I said doubtfully. It hardly seemed likely that *they* would let a little thing like that stop them from opening the briefcase.

He took it back from me. "Or do you think they wouldn't believe me?" he asked. "After all, at my age I have a right to be forgetful. I even have a paper to prove it!" He spent a little while turning the numbers, then he grew visibly anxious, took his jacket off, and was lost in thought. "Would you believe it, my friend, but I really *have* forgotten the combination! And to top it all, I can't see the numbers properly because my glasses are inside!"

He handed the briefcase back again, for me to try my luck.

He then told me which of his friends had been forbidden to publish, although they had all managed to find a benefactor among those who, on the contrary, *had* to publish in order to fill all the journals and magazines. The benefactors would sign their name under the article for a share of the fee and feel that they were fulfilling their academic duty.

"It's very funny," the Professor said. "Imagine that the chief editor of that philosophical rag of ours slates somebody in such a way that you'd think his poor victim would get hauled up in court, but in the same issue he'll print an important article of his without knowing it's by him because it is signed by one of these benefactors. I'll tell you one thing, when one day historians try and sort all this out, they'll have quite a job on their hands."

"You really think anybody will bother to try and sort it out?" I asked.

"Well, you may be right, people will probably have other things to worry about," he agreed with me. "Ecological problems, food shortages, and so on. I tried to write about this the other day, that we're all living in a fool's paradise and that unless we turn our attention to the real problems of this world, future generations will never forgive us. I kept it all very mild, and did my best to couch it in *their* jargon, so that it was very hazy and ambiguous, but when I showed it to my benefactor he almost had a fit. He said that if he as much as showed the article to anyone he could go and find himself a benefactor in his turn! That's the worst of it," he mused, "when you do succeed in finding someone who is willing to pass your ideas off as his own, you then have to tamper with your ideas to make them look as if they were his. But how the devil are you supposed to do that, since they've given up having ideas long ago?"

I had just turned his gadget to 335 when the lock gave a click and snapped open.

"Of course!" exclaimed the professor. "How could I have forgotten? That's the date when Aristotle opened his famous peripateum in Lyceia." And he presented me with forty pages of a text he had typed with his own hand.

And that is how I had spent my time. In discussion, reading, and sometimes actually writing these texts. After a few months this way of life started to get on my nerves. I have little patience with everyday politics. I wanted to write an essay about the satirist Karel Havlíček Borovský, and my publisher beyond two frontiers had sent me a request for a novel.

When my friend the Protestant priest turned up as one of my visitors and I complained that I could not work in peace at home in Prague, he invited me to spend some time in his village.

The village lay just a few miles from the Austrian border. Everybody watched Viennese TV, if they watched anything at all. According to the priest, people switched their sets on and immediately fell asleep, particularly if the news was on. Thanks to this, nobody knew anything about Charter 77 as yet.

"Out there you'll get a splendid rest," he assured me, looking down at me from his six feet three. "Nobody's going to disturb you, at most our reform school girls will coo at you or you'll get a visit from Charles and Luke. They're a trifle...." He used sign language to indicate that these two were not, as they say, all there. "But maybe they'll interest you more than ordinary people—sometimes I think that souls such as these have been granted a special kind of vision."

Well, as far as peace and quiet was concerned, there was more than enough of it here, and to spare. I listened a lot to foreign radio stations and read about Havlíček, who a hundred and thirty years ago had written about the need for just the kind of rights my friends were today demanding in vain.

Once a week I attended Bible classes and stayed for a youth meeting. After a religious lesson, which bored me, they played games, and those I enjoyed. Luke, his feeble-minded appearance notwithstanding, put together a quiz which was almost surrealistic. One of the questions was: Can man be bricked up alive in the fourth dimension?

Sometimes I would go for a long walk around the village. It had only ninety dwellings, but its last house had as its neighbour the first cottage of the next one. Here they had a big glassworks where they produced glasses and tumblers of all

kinds, as well as the delicate figurines which filled my room in
the widow's cottage. The glassworks was so ancient and its
workers so atrociously paid that even in this badly impoverished area they were unable to find enough of them, and so
they brought in "fallen" girls picked up by the police all over
the country and sentenced to reform school training. The
girls lived in a shabby hostel, worked hard for a ridiculous
wage, shouted at every male in sight, and were always trying
to escape.

I got to know one of these girls quite well, because she came
to the rectory in her spare time to be instructed by my friend
in the boundless grace of God, in return for which she helped
his wife in the kitchen or in the garden.

She was quite obviously at least partly of gipsy origin and
rejoiced in a truly Biblical name, Magdalen. I could not tell
how open she was to the grace of God, but whenever she was
left alone with me she would press against me and whisper,
"How about a bit of the other?"

I finished my breakfast. It was a quarter to nine, and outside
the rain continued, grey and endless. I put on a pair of rubber
boots, a raincoat with a hood, and went to church.

The service had just started, my friend's wife was playing
the organ while he sat behind the table in his black garments,
singing. The congregation, I had noticed, consisted either of
the very old (whom I did not know too well) or the very
young. I was practically the only representative of the middle
generation. This time, however, the rain had washed away
even most of the regulars—apart from a few old women I saw
only the familiar faces of the two feeble-minded young men.
Luke, as usual, was sitting in the front row, ready to take
down every word my friend the priest uttered, and Charles,
who suffered from hallucinations, sat alone in the very last
row, handsome, dark-eyed, his emaciated visage covered with
a Christ-like beard. As I entered, they both stared at me, Luke
in glowing friendship, while Charles hunched his shoulders as
if he had seen a devil come in. I took my place in a pew by the

door and tried to find the right psalm in the songbook, although I normally do not sing and find it difficult to concentrate on the lyrics of religious songs.

We were just rising for prayers when the door creaked again and the fallen Magdalen slipped inside. She looked around her, stood for a moment as if in devotion and then, waggling her bottom, made a beeline for me. She was wearing a white nylon blouse, which had become almost transparent as it got wet in the rain, affording a good view of that part of her body which can be described as two young gazelles, to use a suitable simile in this place of worship. Above them glittered a string of the cheapest beads.

Magdalen nudged me with her hip, opened her mouth and licked her lips before moving them as if in prayer. I, however, well knew what it was I would have heard if her voice had been audible.

And so we stood there, praying and begging for the Lord's mercy. I did my best to avert my eyes from the all but naked breasts of my fellow supplicant. I would have liked to have known more about her, how she had sinned and why she had made a habit of coming here to a place most of the other girls did not even know existed.

She noticed me looking at her and tried to read the open Bible over my shoulder. I pushed the book towards her so she could read for herself, and she rewarded me by leaning against me with one of the gazelles.

My friend was reading the lesson of Lazarus and the rich man who could not enter the kingdom of heaven. He was a good preacher. He was trying to explain to the assembled old ladies, the two feeble-minded young men, the fallen Magdalen, his wife, and me that riches were not so much possessions as the relationship of man towards chattels and other people. A man could own very little and yet, by loving things more than human beings and serving them more than the Lord himself, cut himself off from the kingdom of God. He went on to speak of our world of today, in which more and more people lived for material things, caring little for those who suffer, those who are persecuted and sinned against (he was looking towards us as he spoke, and I could not tell if he meant me or my neighbour, or possibly both), concerned only about a new refrigerator or washing machine, a bigger TV set or a garage for their car. All the time they seek new things until one day, in the midst of their material cares, death comes upon them. And if at that moment a judge were to ask them, why did you live, what did you live for, what could they answer? "And do we not believe, do we not know that when our Lord comes to judge the living and the dead He will ask just such a question? None of us will escape His judgement, none will avoid the question. But what shall we answer?"

And when he had appealed to us all to think carefully about our answer, my young friend finished his sermon, and we sang one last song.

All the time the priest was talking, the feeble-minded Luke scribbled in his notebook (his feeble-mindedness, I realised, manifested itself by his eccentric behaviour rather than stupidity), the old women dozed off or nodded their heads occasionally, the mad Charles listened to voices only he could hear, the fallen Magdalen devoured the priest with her eyes, and I—if I tried to describe my feelings I would have to say that I was aware of the presence of order and rejoiced that I, too, had a part to play in it, that I, too, was being addressed as one of the congregation, as a human being.

I had lately felt like an outcast, expelled from every community, unless I were to count the community of those who had been similarly cast out. They had tried to prevent me from addressing anyone, deprived me of my audience—and my audience had naturally not spoken out on my behalf.

Two days earlier we had talked at the rectory about the lack of support for priests who were barred from carrying out their vocation by the authorities, how few people would speak out in their favour. We ended up talking about Havlíček, who had remained quite isolated after his return from exile. And when he died, a hundred and twenty-one years ago, only a handful of friends dared to attend his funeral.

Our nation, said my friend, was not worthy of Havlíček then and is not worthy now of those who are fighting for its rights.

I would not care to pass so harsh a judgement on my nation. In the last few years I have been to several funerals of those who can be described as fighting for the nation's rights. At each of them a great number of people gathered, and every time there were official representatives filming us, during the latest one they even gunned their motorcycle engines behind the cemetery wall so that we should not hear the priest or any other speaker. Someone, they say, placed a crown of thorns on the coffin, just as at Havlíček's funeral. I don't know if this is true, for the crowd was so huge that I could not get near the coffin. And in any case, I read in one biography that the crown of thorns Božena Němcová was supposed to have placed on Havlíček's coffin only turned up in popular mythology later. People need crowns of thorns just as they need martyrs—some to invoke them, others to confess to their shame that they are unworthy of them.

When we left the church I discovered that the rain had stopped, though the sky was still bedecked with low, grey tatters of cloud. My young friend was standing by the church door, bending over to say a few words to each old lady as she left and to shake her hand. I waited for him so I could compliment him on his sermon. Magdalen waited with me, not having anywhere else to go, and the two young men waited too, being used to attract the priest's attention. In any event, they had been promised the kingdom of heaven, quite explicitly, and I thought justly.

As soon as my young friend had said farewell to the last old lady, the young man with the Christ-like face spoke to him: "Oh, Reverend, that was terrible—they kept hissing all the time! I wanted to listen to you, but they wouldn't be quiet. They kept hissing and crawling all around me."

"Who crawled and hissed, Charlie?" asked my friend, nodding to me and the fallen Magdalen.

I knew that Charles was not a local boy, he came here only for the summer to visit his uncle. He was twenty years old and when he was better, he worked as a compositor. (Come to think of it, if I had to set the kind of stuff that was being printed these days, who knows how I would have ended up?)

"I wanted them to bite me," continued Charles. "I so wanted that, because someone has to suffer it."

"It seems to me, Charlie," said my friend, "that you had a most unpleasant dream."

"No, I didn't, Reverend," insisted the young man with the face of Christ. "I saw it."

"Charles," put in Luke, smiling his eternal smile, "don't you think he'll perish?"

"No, I don't," replied the other young man, "it is a monster, its eyes gleam, horrible eyes. He wants to bite each and every one of us until he gets his sacrifice."

"It seems to me, Charlie," said my friend the priest as we made our way along the wet asphalt road towards the rectory, "that you've had some more of your suicidal thoughts."

"Yes, you know, you know," assented the young man, "that I wish to die. Someone has to take it upon himself, and it has to be a very slow and dreadful death, so that mankind should be redeemed, the serpent isn't enough, I want to be crucified! That must be a terrible, physical pain. And all that spitting—people spat at him, Jesus Christ, Reverend, what a guy he must have been, that Christ, all those people spitting at him and he prayed for them!" His face took on such a pained expression as if someone were already nailing him to the cross.

"But, you see, Christ was crucified also to prevent your being spat upon," said my friend the priest, somewhat simplifying the Christian message. "He redeemed you and took all your horrors upon himself."

"Sure, the crucifixion was a fantastic thing, and always will be," said Charles.

"Reverend, did you know," Luke butted in, his face beaming as if he were telling us a joke. "that I too wanted to kill myself? I wanted to poison myself because there isn't a decent idea in the world which someone wouldn't have thought of already. But I don't want to die any more, I want to pass my state exams."

"That's right, Luke," my friend said approvingly, "we all live in hope."

Luke was not kidding about the exams. They had accepted him at the secondary school, first because his parents were glass workers and because that diseased brain of his housed a mathematical genius. Luke could solve the most complicated equations out of his head, and he could not understand why other people were unable to imagine four-dimensional space when it seemed like child's play to him.

Charles was silently following a crack in the road surface, and for a little while no one spoke.

Luke smiled at us, and so did the fallen Magdalen.

But while Luke was smiling a private smile, or again one intended for the whole world, Magdalen was smiling at *me* and giving me a come-hither look with her eyes. Or so at least I thought.

Charles returned to us. "What use will certificates be to you?" he asked logically. "You can't take education with you to the grave."

"Now, Charlie, don't be unkind!" my friend reproved him.

"Please, Reverend," said Luke, who I had heard had been given the lowest marks in all the other subjects, "couldn't we form a group for you to explain some theological concepts? I, for example, don't know what love is. Or atonement."

"I've got mud at home," said Charles.

"Mud? What kind of mud do you have, Charlie?" asked my friend, and I had to admire his patience.

"Rheumatic," explained Charles. "I sleep in it, and that's my atonement."

"Is that right, Reverend?" asked Luke, delighted at this simple definition.

"Well, it is not that simple, lads," said my friend the priest, quite rightly leaving Magdalen and me out of it. "One of these days we'll really have to discuss it."

We came to the crossroads where our ways parted, and here we could see the flooded landscape by the brook. The waters had risen incredibly during the time we had been in church.

Strangely enough, it did not seem frightening to me, but really quite enthralling. I had never seen a flood before. True, I had written a story about one when I was just a boy, but as with all my stories at that time, I had made it all up.

We stopped and stood still, but Charlie immediately hopped across to the water-filled ditch, where he halted, gazing at the flooded countryside. "I do believe He'll come!" he exclaimed in a sudden visionary trance. "I think He's coming!" He stretched an arm out towards the deluged meadows, his gesture so persuasive that we all involuntarily looked in that direction.

"Now whom do you see, Charlie?" asked my friend the priest.

"Why, Him, of course!" exclaimed the young man. "He is striding across the waters and nothing can stop Him. Because He is love! He's wearing a white robe, and there's a crown of thorns upon His head. There, look—over there!"

And we all stared at the expanse of still waters ahead of us. I cannot say what the others saw, but I only saw a seagull sailing above the waters, and I felt a deep sorrow that I had not been vouchsafed the gift of seeing the invisible, of divining the future, that I would probably never catch sight of someone who would bring me solace or a message of love.

Then we parted. I went back to the cottage, where nothing was mine and no one was waiting for me. My friend, meanwhile, strode back to his rectory, happily surrounded by his blessed flock.

At home, I quickly changed and then threaded my careful

way among the glass figurines to sit down at the table. But I had no inclination either to read or write. I was conscious of alien voices, of a strange, excited expectation. This could have been due to the flood, or perhaps I had been affected by the mad, prophetic trance of that Christ-like young man; I found myself actually *expecting* something unusual and portentous to happen.

I had always thought that every prophet must be something of a madman. A normal person, after all, is concerned with things and objects, whereas a prophet deals in visions.

Though it is true that every now and again a prophet may carry the multitude with him, so that, for a while, it will enthusiastically share his vision. And because one of the differences between normal people and visionaries is that the normal ones actually *do* things, the masses set about putting the vision into practice. Inevitably, it all ends with a return to the world of material things, which are now revered more than ever, and with the stoning of the prophets.

This is an eternal cycle, the struggle between matter and spirit, base materialism and naive dreams, the desire to own things and to come to terms with something that is higher than man.

I am in sympathy with the naive dreams of the prophets. I am on their side, even though I know that they will ever suffer ridicule, contempt, and will repeatedly be misunderstood. Yet it was they who, way back in times of old, understood what today is becoming realised even by the less far-seeing: that the mania for possessing things and humiliating the world instead of acquiring humility oneself, will in the end divorce man from the sources of life.

I rose from the table. It was time I did something about my lunch. As I passed the window I caught sight of a rowboat gliding towards me across the lake that had formed in the meadow behind the cottage. The boat passed the house of the football coach, and by the time it reached the bit of dry land a little distance from my cottage, I recognised Magdalen behind the oars. She jumped out and came running towards me. I again carefully negotiated the glass figurines and shelves full of vases and opened the door.

"Hi there!" she shouted, beckoning me to come and join her.

So I put my boots on again, by which time she had reached the cottage, to tell me that over at the rectory they had spotted a man stranded on the other side of the brook, across the bridge, where the road was almost completely submerged by now. The man was obviously not a local, he did not seem to know which way to go, and was lugging a huge suitcase. The priest had sent her to rescue the poor fellow, and did I want to come along?

"Are you good at rowing?" I asked her. "I expect the current will be pretty fierce over there in the hollow."

"I used to row a lot at home," she said. "But if you'd like to have a little fun before we go...," she giggled, misunderstanding my motive. I quickly offered to help her row.

We took our places in the boat, with me taking the oars. She pointed the way. I rowed past the football coach's house and was astonished to see how high the water had risen—we were almost level with the ground floor windowsills. For the first time I was able to see the vast jumble of things inside the cottage—metal pipes running along the walls, and painted wooden chests, and South Bohemian madonnas, and several Christs on the Cross hanging there next to one another as in some religious store.

I sometimes think that man's acquisitive urge is not just the result of his instinctive need to guard against poverty and hunger. It is rather that he wishes to extend his own life in time. But how is he to do that?

By means of an idea encapsulated in some act of creation, by means of an act or object that he himself has fashioned, or at least owned. Most of us, of course, are not creative and there is less opportunity, rather than more, for action, apart from which most human actions vanish without trace faster than man himself. What then is left? Man knows he must die and wants to leave behind a pyramid or at least a house or a bed piled with eiderdowns and a few glass figurines.

Prophets, philosophers and artists have their visions to leave behind, and so they rarely understand this desire on the part of others. The others, in turn, cannot understand that those who are able to extend themselves in time by their ideas or creative acts do not feel this need to own and accumulate objects. If they think about it at all, they find their behaviour incomprehensible, explaining it away as craziness or imputing false motives such as disguised greed or thirst for power.

They cannot understand a Socrates, a Jesus, a Hus, or a Havlíček, and as often as not they will kill him or at least expel him from their midst. The failure to understand persists even when the prophets have long been dead, even when they themselves have come to adopt their legacy and pity them for the poverty or exile they had to endure. They do not see that those whom they consider martyrs were most probably happy, or at least no less happy than their contemporaries who possessed the things they desired.

"Who was it who saw the man?" I asked Magdalen.

"It was him, Charlie," she replied. "The others didn't believe him at first, but then the Reverend fetched a pair of binoculars and he saw him too."

I again felt a strange excitement. In an effort to dispel it, I asked her: "Where do you come from, Magdalen?"

"I come from near Hradec," said the girl. She took off her soaked tennis shoes, rested her feet against my knees, and giggled.

"Been here long?"

"My second year."

"Don't you feel lonely?"

"Lonely?" She seemed surprised by the question. "I feel better here than I ever did at home." Her voice was resonant and coarse. If I did not know what she looked like, I would have thought she was twice her age. She pulled a cigarette from her pocket. She offered me another, but I explained that I didn't smoke and even if I did, I could not while rowing.

We had left the football coach's house behind, with all its painted chests, and were approaching the original site of the brook. The sun slipped out briefly from behind the clouds. Magdalen sent a puff of smoke up towards it and gave a contented sigh.

"Have you a family back home?"

"Yeah." She explained that her father drove a tractor and her mother looked after the cows. Her mother was a gipsy, but only a half-caste. When she dyed her hair, her daughter said proudly, no one could tell that she was dark. Also all her kids were fair, only Magdalen had missed out and looked like a real gipsy. And as there were seven of the fair siblings that preceded her, her father would never believe that this eighth, dusky child was his, and he wanted to get rid of her as soon as she was born.

"But your mother wouldn't let him?"

"Well, the bitch didn't want to lose the child allowance, did she?" My companion giggled again. "But make no mistake, she hated me being dark, no less than he did. She beat me as soon as look at me, they both did."

Then Magdalen told me how she was still in her last year at school when she moved in with Jára the railwayman and showed up at home only occasionally. Her parents didn't mind, she said, because they still claimed her allowance, and that was all they cared about. Then, one winter day, when she visited her old home, she borrowed her mother's coat to go out into the frost. "Just a rag it was, with its sleeves filthy with cow dung," she described it, and I realised that this coat was to play an important role in her future life. "The collar was goat skin, nobody would give you a tenner for it, but Mum went straight to the cops and told 'em I'd pinched it. And would you believe it, she said it was worth one and a half thousand!" This was obviously adding insult to injury where Magdalen was concerned. "She only said that because she thought I'd taken the coat so as to sell it and that she could then get some money out of me. But when they caught me I still had it on. I told them they were crazy, I'd only borrowed it, but they still sent me up for trial. And the lady prosecutor yelled at me that I was nothing but a parasite. Made me out to be a prostitute, she did, and all this time I'd been living with Jára and he'd have knocked my block off if I'd gone with other men.''

''And they found you guilty?''

''I got sent up, and then shipped here.''

''Didn't you appeal?''

''No, I was glad to be free of 'em.''

I was not sure who ''they'' were, whether her parents or the court, probably both. ''And what about your boyfriend?'' I asked?

''Well, what was he to do when I was doing time?'' she demanded, looking up at the sky where the clouds were scattering and startled birds were flying to and fro. ''He wrote that he was still thinking of me but that I mustn't be angry with him, that he had had to find someone else. This is a present from him,'' she showed me the string of cheap, coloured beads. I said how nice, and she went on to tell me how she had cried, but the other girls told her not to be an idiot, that the world was full of men. But here there wasn't a real man in sight, all those at the glassworks were as old as Methuselah, and all they thought about on these hot days was beer.

''So you don't like it here much,'' I concluded, as I rowed towards the woods. All around us was water, I could not even tell whether we were passing over a meadow or a field. It was a magnificent sight, there was something primeval and superhuman about this landscape, and I felt that I had been taken out of time. As if I had been touched by eternity, or God, or justice. Oddly enough, my companion did not disturb this exalted mood of mine—she too seemed to have been touched by eternity.

We safely negotiated the brook, and when we got to the other side I saw a narrow strip of road in the midst of all those waters, and even this was flooded in places. And there, too far for me to make out his features, a man with a suitcase was sitting on one of the milestones.

"I like it everywhere," Magdalen was saying. "As long as I don't see that old bitch of a mother of mine. What was she thinking of? I was going to bring that bloody coat back, wasn't I? But at least she lost her child allowance," she said with relish, "she could still have claimed it for another half year." The sun again peeped out from behind the clouds, and she leaned back in her seat and closed her eyes.

The man had spotted us by now and got up from his perch, standing on the little area of dry land and jumping up and down and waving his arms in the air and shouting at us like a marooned sailor. I could now make out his features, and I also recognised the piece of luggage he had with him—no suitcase but a large, new, shiny briefcase. My throat contracted with emotion as I called out to him: "We're coming, Professor!"

We rescued the professor, his shoes sodden, trousers rolled up above his knees, his whole small frame shaking with cold and his ordeal in general.

I had no sooner sat down at the oars again than he leaned across and whispered that he had brought me a whole lot of wonderful texts and declarations, a list of banned writers, and a list of the new Charter signatories, he had had all this for almost a week, not knowing what to do, but then he said to himself that I must be dying to know what was going on in Prague, and so he took the train and here he was. "Only, the sun has been shining in Prague these last two days, and here I find this catastrophe. I first thought I'd make it along that road, but the water kept rising right in front of my eyes."

"Did you not forget the code this time?" I asked, having first thanked him for taking so much trouble to bring the papers to me.

"No, I didn't," he replied, gleefully. "This time I thought of a splendid number." Leaning close, he whispered the number so that no one else could hear. "You know, the date when

Carneades of Cyrene launched his magnificent series of lectures in Rome. It's an easy one to memorise, and I don't expect *they* would know the date. Don't you agree?''

''Oh, I'm sure they don't,'' I assured him, rowing for all I was worth towards the football coach's house.

As we neared terra firma again I saw a round object floating in the water. I stopped rowing and all three of us tried to make out what it was. Until at last the professor said: ''Why, it's a spinning wheel!''

Now I could see that the water had forced one of the windows open, so that a whole flood of objects came floating out of the football coach's house—there, rocking gently on the waves, was a painted wooden bowl, and a wooden sign which said Home Sweet Home, and the painted doors of a wardrobe, and finally out of the window came a large antique chair. We sat there and watched it being carried slowly towards us. Just as it was about to pass our rowboat, a white seagull came flying down from the sky and perched on its back, surveying the wide expanse of water around him like a captain on his bridge.

The professor leaned towards me again and whispered: ''I can't stand it any longer. I'd like to read something to you— do you think it's all right in front of the girl?''

I assured him it was, but the professor shook his head. ''My glasses are in the briefcase, and I can't see the numbers without them.''

And so I entrusted the oars to Magdalen and picked up the professor's briefcase. ''What's the number?'' I asked.

''But I told you,'' he said, startled. ''Didn't I?''

''You told me about those Roman lectures,'' I admitted, ''but I never studied philosophy. Well, not in any systematic way,'' I corrected myself for accuracy's sake, since I had once upon a time attended a few talks on the subject.

''I didn't tell you the date?'' The professor sounded astonished. ''And I was so glad that I didn't have to keep it in my head.''

He stopped speaking and was lost in thought, while we

floated past an army drum and trumpet, a breadboard with mother-of-pearl edges, a Příbram madonna with a golden crown on her head, and a small jewel box with heaven knows what treasures inside it. All we had to do was to stretch out a hand.

"Wouldn't you like any of this?" I asked Magdalen.

She gave me a surprised look. "What would I do with it? It's all soaking wet."

And now I understood that by some miracle we three were well met in that rowboat.

The professor was all this time whispering to himself, reciting names such as Chrysippos and Philon of Larissa, and then he turned to me again and said that he made it the year 156.

I was tempted to ask whether BC or AD, but was afraid that he might be offended. And so I turned the numbers to 156, and we both waited with bated breath to see whether the briefcase would open.

New and Forthcoming Books
from
READERS INTERNATIONAL

Sipho Sepamla, *A Ride on the Whirlwind*. This novel by one of South Africa's foremost black poets is set in the 1976 Soweto uprisings. "Not simply a tale of police versus rebels," said *World Literature Today*, "but a bold, sincere portrayal of the human predicament with which South Africa is faced." Hardback, 244 pages, summer 1984. Retail price, US$12.50/£7.95 (UK).

Yang Jiang, *A Cadre School Life: Six Chapters*. Translated by Geremie Barmé and Bennett Lee. A lucid, personal meditation on the Cultural Revolution, the ordeal inflicted on 20 million Chinese, among them virtually all of the country's intellectuals. "Yang Jiang is a very distinguished old lady; she is a playwright; she translated Cervantes into Chinese . . . She lived through a disaster whose magnitude paralyzes the imagination . . . She is a subtle artist who knows how to say less to express more. Her *Six Chapters* are written with elegant simplicity." (Simon Leys, *The New Republic*) "An outstanding book, quite unlike anything else from 20th-century China . . . superbly translated." (*The Times Literary Supplement*). Hardback, 91 pages, autumn 1984. Retail price, $9.95/£6.50

Sergio Ramírez, *To Bury Our Fathers*. Translated by Nick Caistor. A panoramic novel of Nicaragua in the Somoza era, dramatically recreated by the country's leading prose artist. Cabaret singers, exiles, National Guardsmen, guerillas, itinerant traders, beauty queens, prostitutes and would-be presidents are the characters who people this sophisticated, lyrical and timeless epic of resistance and retribution. Hardback, 253 pages, early 1985. Retail price $14.95/£9.95. Paperback, $8.95/£5.95

Antonio Skármeta, *I Dreamt the Snow Was Burning*. Translated by Malcolm Coad. A cynical country boy comes to Santiago to win at football and lose his virginity. The last days before the 1973 Chilean coup turn his world upside down. "With its vigour and fantasy, undoubtedly one of the best pieces of committed literature to emerge from Latin America," said *Le Monde*. Hardback, ca.225 pages, spring 1985. Retail price, $14.95/£8.95

Yahya Yakhluf, *Najran Below Zero*. Translated by Marilyn Booth. A tour de force, banned throughout most of the Arab world, that explores the mind of religious fundamentalism. The book demonstrates the dissenting role of the Palestinian intellectual. During years of civil war, the people of the border region of Najran are buffeted /between intimidation and resistance, between Saudi religious repression and an infant Yemeni republic—always with an American presence, hovering and anonymous. Hardback, ca.110 pages, autumn 1985. Retail price, $12.50/£7.95

READERS INTERNATIONAL publishes contemporary literature of quality from Latin America and the Caribbean, the Middle East, Asia, Africa and Eastern Europe. Each of the books in this first annual series was initially banned at home: READERS INTERNATIONAL is particularly committed to conserving literature in danger. Each book is current—from the past 10 years. And each is new to readers here. READERS INTERNATIONAL is registered as a not-for-profit, tax-exempt organisation in the United States of America.

If you wish to know more about Readers International's series of contemporary world literature, please write to 503 Broadway, 5th Floor, New York, NY 10012, USA; or to the Editorial Branch, 8 Strathray Gardens, London NW3 4NY, England. Orders in North America can be placed directly with Readers International, Subscription/Order Department, P.O. Drawer E, Columbia, Louisiana 71418, USA.